W9-BGI-405

Women's Work in Nineteenth-Century London

WOMEN'S WORK
IN NINETEENTH-CENTURY LONDON
A Study of the Years 1820-50

by

Sally Alexander

The Journeyman Press, *London & West Nyack*
and the London History Workshop Centre

The Journeyman Press Limited, 97 Ferme Park Road, Crouch End, London N8 9SA, and 17 Old Mill Road, West Nyack, NY 10994, USA

The London History Workshop Centre, Mary Ward Centre, Queen Square, London WC1

First published in *The Rights and Wrongs of Women,* edited and introduced by Juliet Mitchell and Ann Oakley, 1976

Reprinted 1983 by the Journeyman Press Limited and the London History Workshop Centre

Copyright © Sally Alexander, 1983

ISBN 0 904526 82 8

All rights reserved. No part of this publication may be reproduced, stored in a retrieval system, or transmitted, in any form or by any means, electronic, mechanical, photocopying, recording or otherwise, without the prior permission of the publishers.

The publishers would like to thank the Film and History Project 'The Song of the Shirt' for their illustrations reproduced in this book.

Printed in Great Britain

Contents

Introduction

Most historians define the working class *de facto* as working men. Occupations, skills, wages, relations of production, the labour process itself, are discussed as if social production were an exclusively male prerogative. Consciously or unconsciously, the world has been conceived in the image of the bourgeois family – the husband is the breadwinner and the wife remains at home attending to housework and child-care. Both the household itself, and women's domestic labour within it are presented as the unchanging backcloth to the world of real historical activity. The labour historian has ignored women as workers – on the labour market and within the household. Consequently women's contribution to production and as well to the reproduction and maintenance of the labour force has been dismissed. This is partly because the labour and economic historians who first wrote about the working class, wrote about the organized and articulate labour movement – accessible through its trade union records, its newspapers and the occasional autobiography. Only recently have the inaccessible areas of working-class life been approached, but even here the focus has remained on the working man. In every respect women's participation in history has been marginalized.[1]

Feminist history releases women from their obscurity as the wives, mothers and daughters of working men. This does not just mean that family life, housework, the reproduction of the labour force, the transmission of ideology etc. can be added to an already constituted history, but the history of production itself will be rewritten. For the history of production under capitalism, from a

7

feminist perspective, is not simply the class struggle between the producer and the owner of the means of production. It is also the development of a particular form of the sexual division of labour in relation to that struggle.

The focus of this article is women's waged work in London in the early Victorian period. London in the period of the industrial revolution has been chosen for two reasons. Firstly, because it offers a wide survey of women's employments within a reasonably manageable geographic unit; and because it illustrates the multiple effects of industrial change on women's work, reminding us that the industrial revolution brought with it more than just machinery and the factory system. But first, a discussion of some of the limitations of the conventional sources for women's employment in the Victorian period will remind us that the labour historian is not the original villain – the problem begins with the sources themselves.

*

The working woman emerged as a 'social problem' in the thirties and forties. Indeed, it is as though the Victorians discovered her, so swiftly and urgently did she become the object of public concern. The dislocations of modern industry, the rapid increase in population, the herding of the population into the towns, dramatized class antagonisms and forced the condition of the working classes onto the attention of the propertied class as a mass of documentary evidence reveals. The effect of these dislocations upon working-class wives and children became one major focal point of this anxiety. The short-time movement (the struggle of the factory operatives in the Lancashire and Yorkshire textile mills to limit the working day), in particular Sadler's Commission of 1832, first highlighted the problem of the female factory operative. Ten years later, the Children's Employment Commission (1842–3) exposed a string of female occupations in the mines and the traditional outwork trades, where wages and conditions were no less degrading than those in the textile mill. These revelations shattered middle-class complacency and aroused the reformatory zeal of Evangelical and Utilitarian philanthropists. And it is from the philanthropists, as well as

8

factory inspectors, that we receive most of our information on women's work.

This sense of shock at 'the condition of England', as contemporaries termed it, in particular the apparent destruction of the working-class family, cannot be understood simply from the terrible conditions in the factories alone.[2] The British Industrial Revolution did not take place in a neutral political context. Its formative years, 1790 to 1815, were years in which England was engaged in counter-revolutionary war against France. Jacobinism (the ideology of the French Revolutionaries) and industrial discontent were fused by England's rulers into an indiscriminate image of 'sedition'. Any political or industrial activity among the working classes was severely repressed. Out of this repression emerged the distinctive features of Victorian middle-class ideology – a blend of political economy and evangelicalism. The one an ideology appropriate to the 'take off' of the forces of production – the industrial revolution; the other a doctrine demonstrating the fixity of the relations of production. While political economy asserted that the laws of capitalist production were the laws of nature herself, evangelicalism sanctified the family, along with industriousness, obedience and piety, as the main bulwark against revolution. The Victorian ideal of womanhood originated in this counter-revolutionary ideology. The woman, as wife and mother, was the pivot of the family, and consequently the guardian of all Christian (and domestic) virtues. Women's waged work, therefore, was discussed insofar as it harmonized with the home, the family and domestic virtue.

Because of women's very special responsibility for society's well-being, it was the woman working outside the home who received most attention from the parliamentary commissioners, and to push through legislative reform, emphasis was placed, not on the hours of work, rates of pay, and dangers from unsafe machinery – although all these were mentioned – but on the moral and spiritual degradation said to accompany female employment; especially the mingling of the sexes and the neglect of domestic comforts. 'In the male the moral effects of the system are very sad, but in the female they are infinitely worse', Lord Shaftesbury solemnly declared to a silent House of Lords, at the end of his two-hour speech advocating the abolition of women and children's work in the mines . . . 'not alone upon themselves, but upon their families, upon society, and, I may add, upon the country itself. It is bad enough if you corrupt the man, but if you corrupt the woman, you poison the waters of life at the very fountain.'[3]

Respectable opinion echoed Lord Shaftesbury's sentiments. Both evangelicalism and political economy attributed the sufferings of the poor to their own moral pollution. Their viciousness was variously ascribed to drink, licentiousness, idleness and all manner of vice and depravity, for which religion, temperance, thrift, cleanliness, industriousness and self help were advocated as the most potent remedies. But, if there was any reason for these evils – beyond the innate moral depravity of the individuals concerned – the one that commended itself most readily was the negligence and ignorance of the working-class wife and mother. It is true that enlightened public opinion – enlightened, that is, by an acquaintance with the poor acquired through visiting them for religious or reformatory purposes – recognized that the crowded courts, tenements and rookeries of the cities, so deplored by Octavia Hill and her associates, hardly stimulated the domestic virtues nurtured in the suburban villa.[4] Nevertheless, the very squalor of working-class housing could be blamed upon the slender acquaintance with domestic economy possessed by working women whose 'want of management' drove their husbands to the alehouses and their children onto the streets. The remedy was succinctly expressed by Mrs Austin, an ardent advocate of 'industrial' education for the working girl – 'our object', she wrote in the 1850s, 'is to improve the servants of the rich, and the wives of the poor'.[5]

Every Victorian inquiry into the working class is steeped in the ideology we have been discussing. The poor were seldom allowed to speak for themselves. 'What the poor are to the poor is little known,' Dickens wrote in the 1840s, 'excepting to themselves and God.'[6] And if this was true of the poor as a whole, it was doubly true of working-class women who almost disappear under the relentless scrutiny of the middle class. It was not that the Victorians did not expect women of the lower classes to work. On

10

the contrary, work was the sole corrective and just retribution for poverty; it was rather that only those sorts of work that coincided with a woman's natural sphere were to be encouraged. Such discrimination had little to do with the danger or unpleasantness of the work concerned. There was not much to choose for example – if our criteria is risk to life or health – between work in the mines, and work in the London dressmaking trades. But no one suggested that sweated needlework should be prohibited to women. To uncover the real situation of the working woman herself in the Victorian period, then, we have to pick our way through a labyrinth of middle-class moralism and mystification and resolve questions, not only that contemporaries did not answer, but in many cases did not even ask.

*

This applies in particular to women's employment in London. Some trades it is true, received a great deal of local attention. The declining Spitalfields silk industry was investigated as part of the national inquiries into the hand-loom weavers; dressmakers and needlewomen received the notice of a House of Lords Select Committee; while starving needlewomen and prostitutes were the subject of a host of pamphlets. But the factory girls of Manchester and the West Riding who so traumatized observers in the 1840s could have no place in London where few trades were transformed by the factory system until the twentieth century. (The high cost of rent in central London combined with the high cost of fuel and its transportation, inhibited the earlier development of the factory system.) What changes did occur in the sexual division of labour as a result of a change in the production or labour process, took place beneath the surface, in the workshop, or the home. Most women workers in London were domestic servants, washerwomen, needlewomen or occupied in some other sort of home work. Many married women worked with their husbands in his trade. These traditional forms of women's work were quite compatible with the Victorian's deification of the home, and so passed almost unnoticed.

Material proof that women's work was not just less noticeable in London but often completely overlooked is found in the

11

Census of 1851. The number of women over twenty who are listed as being without occupation is 432,000, i.e. 57 per cent of all women over twenty living in London. In round numbers, this figure of 432,000 is broken down as follows: 317,000 wives 'not otherwise described', 27,000 widows 'not otherwise described', 43,000 children and relatives at home 'not otherwise described', 26,000 persons of rank or property, 7,000 paupers, prisoners and vagrants, 13,000 'of no specified occupations or conditions'.[7] If we exclude the 26,000 propertied at one end, the 7,000 paupers etc., at the other, and a proportion of propertied widows and dependent relatives in between, that still leaves over 50 per cent of women 'with no occupation'. And yet among the vast majority of the working class, all members of the family were expected to contribute to the family income, for even when the wages of the male workers were relatively high they were rarely regular.[8] We know therefore that 50 per cent of adult women would not have been able to live without any independent source of income. Obviously the statistics require explanation.

There were several reasons why the occupations of working-class women might not have been declared in the Census, some more speculative than others. The work of married women for instance, was often hidden behind that of their husbands. Alice Clark, Dorothy George and Ivy Pinchbeck have shown that although the separation of workplace and home (introduced by merchant capitalism) was one of the factors reducing the opportunities for women to learn a skill or to manage a small workshop business, nevertheless, the process was gradual, especially in the numerous and diverse London trades which, well into the nineteenth century, were characteristically conducted in small workshops, often on a family basis. Some women were listed in the Census as innkeepers', shopkeepers', butchers', bakers' and shoemakers' etc. wives; but often a wife's connection with her husband's trade would not have been mentioned. Many trade societies forbad the entry of women. Also, because the head of the household filled in the Census, he – especially if he was a skilled artisan or aspiring tradesman – probably thought of his wife as a housewife and mother and not as a worker.[9]

Wives of skilled workmen may be glimpsed, however, through

conversations recorded by Mayhew. Sawyers' wives and children, for instance, did not 'as a general rule . . . go *out* to work', (my italics),[10] and coachmen's wives were not in regular employ for the slop-tailors, because, as one confided in Mayhew, 'we keep our wives too respectable for that'.[11] Nevertheless, according to Mayhew, 'some few of the wives of the better class of workmen take in washing or keep small "general shops"'.[12] Taking in washing, needlework, or other sorts of outwork was the least disruptive way of supplementing the family income when extra expenses were incurred, or during the seasonal or enforced unemployment which existed in most London trades. Home work did not unnecessarily interrupt a man's domestic routine, since the wife could fit it in among her household chores; it simply meant she worked a very long day.

But only a minority of women would have been married to skilled artisans or small tradesmen. Mayhew estimated that about 10 per cent of every trade were society men, and Edward Thompson has outlined the 30s. line of privilege in London, while suggesting that Mayhew's 10 per cent was probably an exaggeration, 5 or 6 per cent being a more realistic figure.[13] Society men were becoming more and more confined to the 'honourable' sectors of every trade in the 1840s (i.e. those who produced expensive well-made goods for the luxury and West End market), whereas workers in the unorganized, dishonourable sectors were rapidly expanding in the period 1815–40, and they made a much more precarious living. Women (and children) of this class always had to contribute to the family income, indeed, in the 1830s and 1840s, a time of severe economic hardship, the London poor drew more closely together, and it was often the household and not the individual worker, or even separate families, that was the economic unit. A mixture of washing, cleaning, charring as well as various sorts of home- or slop-work, in addition to domestic labour, occupied most women throughout their working lives. The diversity and indeterminancy of this spasmodic, casual and irregular employment was not easily condensed and classified into a Census occupation.

Other women who were scarcely recorded in the Census, though we know of their existence through Mayhew, were the street traders, market workers, entertainers, scavengers, mudlarks;[14] also those who earned a few pence here and there, looking after a neighbour's children, running errands, minding a crossing, sweeping the streets, in fact, most of the women discussed in the final section of this paper. Lastly, perhaps the most desperate source of income for women, and one which provoked a great deal of prurient debate and pious attention was prostitution. This too was often intermittent and supplementary and found no place in the Census.

Despite the fact that working women emerge only fitfully through the filter of Victorian moralism; in spite of the tendency to view women as the wives and dependents of working men rather than workers in their own right; in spite of the particular problems of uncovering women's employment in London; nevertheless, some distinguishing characteristics are beginning to appear.

Firstly, London offered no single staple employment for women comparable to that in the northern textile towns; secondly, in a city of skilled trades and small workshops, women, although long since excluded from formal apprenticeship, often worked with their husband in his trade; thirdly, much women's work outside small workshop production was intermittent and casual, which meant that most women's working lives were spent in a variety of partial occupations most of which escaped the rigid classifications of the Census.

These features of women's work must be looked at against the wider background of the London labour market, and the sexual division of labour within it, but first, to help fix the locality, a brief descriptive sketch of London follows.

London Topography

In 1828, Fennimore Cooper described his journey through the outskirts of London as one through a 'long maze of villages'. Even then the description was a little whimsical. London's first period of expansion had been the late sixteenth and early seventeenth centuries, since when it had continued to extend its influence as the political, commercial and manufacturing centre

14

of England. London was also the largest single consumer market in the country. Between 1801 and 1851 London underwent another burst of expansion; her population increased 150 per cent from 900,000 to 2,360,000. Industrial and commercial innovations were affecting every aspect of its economic life. Railways were transforming not only the topography, but manners, morals, customs, the very tempo of life. London was becoming much more accessible to the rest of Britain. Finally, if industrial productivity and expansion in trade and shipping had made Britain the workshop of the world by 1851, developments in banking, shareholding and company investment were making the City its most important financial centre.

London – world centre of commerce, shipping and trade – does not correspond to the image conjured up by Fennimore Cooper, and yet there was a sense in which London was a rambling collection of hamlets. Certainly, its local government before the 1890s lent reality to that myth, if myth it was. G. L. Gomme, looking at a map of London in the 1830s, suggested it resembled an octopus, the boundary of whose body passed from Vauxhall Bridge, to Park Lane, then followed up the Edgware Road, along Marylebone Road, City Road, then southwards past Mile End, reaching the Thames at Shadwell Basin. Apart from the almost independent enclaves of Greenwich and Deptford, the south of the river began with Bermondsey – separated from Deptford by Rotherhithe. By the middle of the century, according to John Hollingshead, it 'wriggled' its way 'through the existing miles of dirt, vice and crime as far as the Lambeth marshes'. Between 1830 and 1850, London was greedily swallowing up the surrounding villages, and transforming them into the 'stuccovia, the suburbs, the terminus districts', which from the 1840s onwards, appeared with increasing frequency in the novels of Dickens.[15]

The process of incorporation was rapid, but their transformation gradual. The differences and peculiarities of London districts remained very marked. Their geographic, social and economic distinctions were more than the preservation of quaint custom. In 1830 Hampstead, Islington, Hackney and east of Bethnal Green and Stepney were rural or semi-rural. So was south of the river beyond Southwark and Bermondsey. In the early morning the park side of Piccadilly was crowded with women carrying baskets of fruit and vegetables on their heads on their way to Covent Garden from the market gardens of Hammersmith, Fulham and Chelsea, where the river ran through fields.[30] Every street was filled with costers on their way to market. Sophie Wackles in *Great Expectations*, married Mr Chegg, a market gardener from Chelsea.

Between the semi-rural outposts in the north and the north-east, and central London, were waste districts, great tracts of suburban Sahara, such as Dickens described in a walk from the City to the outskirts of Holloway, 'where tiles and bricks were burnt, bones were boiled, carpets were beat, rubbish was shot, dogs were fought, and dust was heaped by contractors'.[16] Hector Gavin in his 'sanitary ramblings' through Bethnal Green in the 1840s similarly found yards for the collection of dust, refuse and ash, overflowing sewers and open drains and other 'nuisances'. These had gradually been encroaching on the plots laid out as gardens where he saw 'the choicest flowers', dahlias and tulips.[17] The railway, that harbinger of progress, left chaos in its wake in outlying parts of the East End – contributing to its general atmosphere of desolation and disease by the destruction of streets and alleys and the accumulation of rubbish yards and dung heaps in their place. The summer houses belonging to the gardens of Bethnal Green were being used for 'human habitation', and every bit of spare ground was being built on: houses that were neither paved or boarded, lacking in sanitation and built below ground level.

Jerry builders were busy throughout suburban London. The hasty conversion of sheds and shacks into homes in Spitalfields, the cheap building in these waste districts of the East End, and on the outskirts of the City – Shoreditch, St Pancras, Agar Town for example, once described as 'a squalid population that had first squatted' – the rows of small houses that were built with 'mere lathe and plaster' purely for quick profit had their central London counterparts in the decaying tenements of the City and the West End, and south of the river in Southwark and Bermondsey.

The intervening waste lands between London and its outlying

16

villages were being depredated and abused on the north and north-east sides of the City – between London and Finchley for instance, or the hills and fields of north Holloway or Hackney, or the semi-rural outpost of Bethnal Green. The west and the north-west had long ago been colonized by the propertied and professional classes. As one moved from west to east, in a sort of arc from Charing Cross, fashionable society gave way to the aspiring and respectable, but definitely lower middle classes. Here, in Somers Town and Camden Town, were the clerks who toiled all day at their desks in the City or the port; whose wives kept up appearances, and whose daughters struggled in select 'seminaries' to acquire such diverse but necessary preparations for marriage as 'English composition, geography, and the use of dumb-bells . . . writing, arithmetic, dancing, music and general fascination . . . the art of needlework, marking and samplery . . .'[18] Further east, drawing inwards towards the City, lived lacemakers, drapers, embroiderers, the straw-hat and bonnet makers and the milliners of Marylebone and St Pancras, the artificial flower makers, bonnet and cap makers of Clerkenwell and St Lukes.

It is the nucleus of London which is the focus of this study: the City and its perimeter, the East End and south of the river from Rotherhithe to Lambeth. Although, in these predominently manufacturing regions of London, the polarization of classes was still far from complete – 'in the Bethnal Green and Whitechapel unions, in which are found some of the worst conditioned masses of population in the metropolis, we also find good mansions, well drained and protected, inhabited by persons in the most favourable circumstances', wrote Chadwick for instance, in his *Sanitary Report*[19] – the migration of the middle classes to the suburbs was under way.

Omnibus and rail were beginning to make possible this migration, but the principal metropolitan trades and manufactures remained in the centre – and the working classes with them. The industrial districts of London had established themselves east of the City and south of the river in the sixteenth century. During the eighteenth and early nineteenth centuries, the ground between the City and the East End had been built over; workshops and warehouses were built in and to the north and east of the City,

17

while docks and shipyards were beginning to stretch eastwards from the Tower. Such changes had pushed many workers out of the City itself, and, between 1700 and 1831, its population dropped from 210,000 to 122,000.[20] By 1800 then, artisans and labourers were well established in the industrial belt encircling the City, and over the river in Southwark and Bermondsey. There they remained in their 'haunts of poverty' and 'pockets of vice' in the first half of the nineteenth century. Railways, docks and other 'improvements' failed to dislodge them. In Whitechapel, for instance, between 1821 and 1851 the population increased from 68,905 to 79,759, although several thousand houses and 14,000 persons had been displaced by the building of the London (1800–1805) and St Katherine's (1828) docks, together with railways and other enterprises. The result was that the 'labouring class' crowded 'themselves into those houses which were formerly occupied by respectable tradesmen and mechanics, and which are now let into tenements'.[21] Further west, the effect of pushing New Oxford Street through one of the most populous districts of St Giles was that whereas in 1840 the houses in Church Lane had twenty-four occupants each, by 1847 they had forty.[22] Indeed, with the exception of parts of Bethnal Green, Mile End Old Town, St Olave's Southwark and southern Lambeth, all the inner industrial perimeter of London was overcrowded, with between fifteen and forty houses per acre – and the population of every district in this area increased between 1831 and 1851.[23]

The overspill of the working classes in central and east London and their relative isolation from the middle classes, even within a particular district, were a source of perpetual anxiety to Victorian philanthropists and utilitarians. Separation of the classes was dangerous since it bred class hatred; proximity of the poor among themselves led to contamination; overcrowding naturally encouraged promiscuity and all manner of depravity. Nevertheless, the poor continued to crowd in on one another because they had to live near their place of work, which in the 1830s and 1840s was still largely localized in the inner industrial perimeter. There were no cheap transport facilities until the last third of the nineteenth century, and much employment was casual – that is, the worker was employed on a day-to-day or weekly basis. Every trade had its casual fringe and in many partial and improvised occupations (of which London, as a capital city, had an abundant supply), employment sometimes only amounted to a few hours a week, and even then was contingent on being immediately accessible. Even workers in the 'honourable trades' had to be 'on call' daily, which meant it was impractical to live further away from the place of work than a couple of miles.

There were working-class communities beyond the industrial perimeter of course – the potteries of Kensington, for instance, colonized by pig-keepers, and later brickmakers, in the early part of the nineteenth century. And, in every wealthy district, 'from Belgravia to Bloomsbury – from St Pancras to Bayswater' – there was

hardly a settlement of leading residences that has not its particular colony of ill-housed poor hanging onto its skirts. Behind the mansion there is generally a stable, and near the stable there is generally a maze of close streets, containing a small greengrocer's, a small dairy's, a quiet coachman's public house, and a number of houses let out in tenements. These houses shelter a large number of painters, bricklayers, carpenters, and similar labourers, with their families, and many laundresses and charwomen.[24]

But while these groups are important in so far as they serve as a reminder that London was the centre of wealth, luxury, fashion and conspicuous consumption – they were part of a different city from the East End, the City and its boundaries north and south of the river.

Within the industrial perimeter and the East End, work specializations on a local basis reinforced the separation into distinctive communities. In the 1850s, Mayhew listed, apart from the Spitalfields silk weavers, 'the tanners of Bermondsey – the watchmakers of Clerkenwell – the coachmakers of Long Acre – the marine store dealers of Saffron Hill – the old clothes men of Holywell Street and Rosemary Lane – the potters of Lambeth – the hatters of the Borough'.[25] More could be added. But the correlation between district and trade was never absolute, except perhaps in a place like Bermondsey, virtually surrounded by

19

water and uninviting to outsiders because of the 'pungent odours' that exuded from the tanneries, glue, soap and other manufactories of the noxious trades. In general, it was poverty and common want that drew people together in the tenements of St Giles's, or parts of the East End, haunts of the poor as Dickens describes in the *Old Curiosity Shop*:

> ... a straggling neighbourhood, where the mean houses parcelled off in rooms, and windows patched with rags and paper, told of the populous poverty that sheltered there ... mangling women, washerwomen, cobblers, tailors, chandlers driving their trades in parlours and kitchens and back-rooms and garrets, and sometimes all of them under the same roof.[26]

The women of these districts are the subject of this essay.

London Trades and the Sexual Division of Labour

Women's waged work was not immediately conspicuous in London in the early Victorian period. Women were not found in the skilled and heavy work in shipbuilding and engineering, two of London's staple industries in the first half of the nineteenth century. Neither were they employed in the docks and warehouses, nor their subsidiary trades. There were no women in the public utilities, (gas, building etc.) or transport, nor in most semi-processing and extractive industries – sugar refining, soap manufacture, blacking, copper and lead working and the 'noxious' trades – which were London's principal factory trades in this period. Finally, women were excluded from the professions, the civil service, clerical work, the scientific trades, and had been excluded from the old guild crafts (e.g. jewellers, precious instrument makers, carriage builders etc.) since the fourteenth and fifteenth centuries. If women were not in the heavy or skilled industries, in public service or factory, in the professions or clerical work, then where were they to be found?

The 1851 Census tells us (in round numbers) that 140,000 women over twenty, (or 18 per cent of women of that age group) were employed in domestic service; 125,000 (16·3 per cent) were in clothing and shoemaking; 11,000 (1·9 per cent) were teachers and 9,000 (1·2 per cent) worked in the silk industry. The bulk of the remainder were employed either in other branches of manufacture, (artificial-flower making, straw-hat and bonnet making, tailoresses, etc.) or as licensed victuallers, shopkeepers, innkeepers and lodging-house keepers, or else they were listed as the wives of tradesmen and manufacturing workers. Bearing in mind the insufficiency of the 1851 Census as a source, we can see that women's work fell into four principal categories: firstly, all aspects of domestic and household labour – washing, cooking, charring, sewing, mending, laundry work, mangling, ironing etc; secondly, child-care, and training; thirdly, the distribution and retail of food and other articles of regular consumption; and finally, specific skills in manufacture based upon the sexual division of labour established when production (both for sale and domestic use) had been organized within the household. That is to say: the sexual division of labour on the labour market originated with, and paralleled that within the family.

This sketch of women's waged work in London is not an over-simplification. A closer examination of the Census and other sources apparently reveals a wider variety of women's work. Arthur J. Munby, for instance, a careful observer of working-class women, wrote in June 1861:

London Bridge, more than any place I know here, seems to be the great thoroughfare for young working women and girls. One meets them at every step: young women carrying large bundles of umbrella frames home to be covered; young women carrying cages full of hats, which yet want the silk and the binding, coster-girls often dirty and sordid, going to fill their empty baskets, and above all female sack-makers.[27]

And in the same year Munby met or noticed female mudlarks, brick-makers, milk-girls, shirt-collar makers, a porter, a consumptive embroiderer, a draper's shop assistant as well as servants and some agricultural labourers from the country. Mayhew also talked with women in heavy manual work: dustwomen, milk-girls, porters, market girls. Nevertheless, most women's work fitted into the categories described above. Poverty had always forced some women to seek employment in heavy, unpleasant, irregular work, especially those women outside the family, or

21

with no male wage coming in regularly. Dorothy George wrote of women among the eighteenth-century London poor, for instance, that there is no work 'too heavy or disagreeable to be done by women provided it is also low paid'.[28] And an investigation by the Statistical Society into the poorer classes in St George's in the East, uncovered the same characteristics of women's employment in 1848. Whereas men's wages

varied as usual, with the degree of skill required in the several trades, the lowest being those of the sailors, 11s. 10d. per week beside rations, and of the mere labourers, 15s. 7d. per week, on the average; the highest those of the gunsmiths, 41s. 9d. per week; the general average being 20s. 2d. per week . . .

The average wage of single women and widows was only 6s. 10d. The average earnings of 'widows with encumbrance' was 9s. 11d. The report blamed those 'limited means' on the 'narrow range of employments available for female hands, especially if unaccompanied by a vigorous frame and habits of bodily exertion'.[29] Although the sexual division of labour was seldom static on the London labour market, the designation 'women's work' always meant work that was unskilled, overcrowded and low paid. Consequently men in the relatively highly paid skilled trades, especially in the honourable sectors, jealously resisted the entry of women into their trades and excluded them from their trade societies. Indeed, such was the force of custom and tradition in the structure of the London labour market that the appearance of women into a previously male-dominated trade or skill indicated a down-grading of the work involved, and this was generally achieved through a change in the production process itself.

The Capitalist Mode of Production and the Sexual Division of Labour

The sexual division of labour – both within and between the London trades – in the 1830s and 1840s had been established in the period of manufacture (roughly from the sixteenth to the eighteenth century). It was predetermined by the division of labour that had existed within the family when the household had

22

An OUTLINE of SOCIETY _ in _ OUR OWN TIMES _

SPECIMENS FROM MR PUNCH'S INDUSTRIAL EXHIBITION OF 1850
(To be improved in 1851)

been the unit of production. The epoch of modern industry, far from challenging this division further demarcated and rigidified it. Historically many steps in this process must be left to the imagination. Its progress anyway varied from trade to trade and was modified by local custom. But a schematic outline can be given of the way in which capitalist production, as it emerged and matured, structured the sexual division of labour.

Capitalist production developed within the interstices of the feudal mode of production; it emerged alongside of, but also in opposition to, small peasant agriculture and independent handicrafts. Capitalist production first manifests itself in the simultaneous employment and cooperative labour of a large number of labourers by one capitalist. Cooperation based on division of labour assumes its characteristic form in manufacture, which, as a mode of production arose from the breakdown of the handicrafts system.[30] Each step in the development of capitalist production is marked by a further refinement in the division of labour, so that what distinguishes the labour process in manufacture from that in handicrafts is that whereas the worker in the latter produces a commodity, the detail labourer in manufacture produces only part of a commodity.[31] Nevertheless, the technical basis of manufacture remains the handicraft skills. However, these skills become differentiated:

Since the collective labourer has functions, both simple and complex, both high and low, his members, the individual labour-powers, require different degrees of training, and must therefore have different values. Manufacture, therefore, develops a hierarchy of labour-powers, to which there corresponds a scale of wages. If, on the one hand, the individual labourers are appropriated and annexed for life by a limited function; on the other hand, the various operations of the hierarchy are parcelled out among the labourers according to both their natural and their acquired capabilities. Every process of production, however, requires certain simple manipulations, which every man is capable of doing. They too are now severed from their connection with the more pregnant moments of activity and ossified into exclusive functions of specially appointed labourers. Hence, Manufacture begets, in every handicraft that it seizes upon, a class of so-called unskilled labourers, a class which handicraft industry strictly excluded. If it develops a one-sided speciality into a perfection, at the expense of the absence of the whole of a man's working capacity, it also begins to make a speciality of the absence of all development. Alongside of the hierarchic gradation there steps the simple separation of the labourers into skilled and unskilled.[32]

The accumulation of capital was held back by the handicraft base of manufacture, which enabled skilled workmen to exert some control over the labour process through combination in a trade society. Entry into the trade was restricted and knowledge of the skills involved in the work process was confined to those who entered formal apprenticeship But these limited privileges were gained at the expense of the 'unskilled'. Excluded from trade societies most workers were denied a specialized training, and hence lacked bargaining power against capital. The transition from handicrafts to manufacture relegated most women to this position.

By the fifteenth century many craft guilds were excluding women, except for the wives and widows of master craftsmen. Even when women were admitted there is little to indicate that they had ever been formally trained in the technical skills of the labour process itself.[33] But the guilds had been organizations of master craftsmen. With the accumulation of capital, and demarcation of economic classes within a handicraft, the practice of a craft or trade required more capital. The proportion of masters to journeymen altered on the one hand, while, on the other, the impoverished craftsmen (masters or journeymen) practised their trade outside the jurisdiction of the guilds. As more journeymen became wage-earners at their masters' workshops, they organized themselves into societies to protect their interests, which, insofar as they preserved work customs etc., coincided with the master craftsmen against the domination of merchant capital and the encroachment of the unskilled. These journeyman societies also excluded women. Women, who were now denied access to socially recognized skills, formed a source of cheap labour power for the unskilled unorganized branches of production developing outside the corporate guilds. This pool of female labour formed one basis of the industrial reserve army, which was at once both a precondition and necessary product of the accumulation of capital.[34]

26

Women's vulnerability as wage-workers stemmed from their child-bearing capacity. Upon which 'natural' foundation the sexual division of labour within the family was based. Because, in its early organization (the putting-out, or domestic system), capitalism seized the household or the family as the economic and often the productive unit, the sexual division of labour was utilized and sustained as production was transferred from the family to the market-place.

The pre-industrial family had a patriarchal structure. This was true of the working-class family in the period of manufacture (sixteenth to eighteenth centuries), whether the family was employed directly on the land or in an urban craft or trade, or in a rural domestic trade. The father was head of the household, his craft or trade most often determined the family's principal source of income, and his authority was sanctioned by both the law of God and the law of Nature. Nevertheless (except among the very wealthy minority), every member of the family participated in production and contributed to the family income. A woman's work in the home was different from her husband's, but no less vital. (All women were married or widowed in the pre-industrial period except for those in service.) Her time was allocated between domestic labour and work in production for sale, according to the family's economic needs. And sometimes a woman's economic contribution to family income was considerable (especially in rural industries). But a wife's responsibility for the well-being of her husband and children always came before her work in social production, and in a patriarchal culture, this was seen to follow naturally from her role in biological reproduction.[35]

The intervention of capitalism into the sexual division of labour within the patriarchal family confirmed the economic subordination of the wife. By distinguishing between production for use and production for exchange and by progressively subordinating the former to the latter, by confining production for use to the private world of the home and female labour, and production for exchange increasingly to the workshop outside the home and male labour, capitalism ensured the economic dependence of women upon their husbands or fathers for a substantial part of their lives. In these conditions, each further step in the develop-

27

ment of capitalist production – breakdown of the handicraft's system, division of labour, exclusion from the skilled craft guilds, separation of workshop and home, formation of trade societies – further undermined women's position on the labour market. Manufacture provided the economic conditions for the hierarchy of labour powers, but it was the transference of the sexual division of labour from the family into social production which ensured that it was women who moved into the subordinate and auxiliary positions, within it. (The other main area of women's employment, domestic and personal service, cannot be analysed in these terms, since it remained outside capitalist production proper arguably into the twentieth century. This did not prevent it however, from sharing the general characteristics of women's work, low pay and low status).

This reservoir of female labour was an immediate source of cheap labour power ready for utilization by capitalist production when a revolution in the mode of production altered the technical base of the labour process. For as long as production depended upon the workman's skilled manipulation of the instruments of labour, the capitalist could not dislodge his skilled workmen. Only the decomposition of that skill into its constituent parts, which was brought about by a revolution in the instruments of labour, could break up workmen's control over the labour process. It was this revolutionary progress in the division of labour which marked the advent of the epoch of modern industry. Machinery and the factory system abolished the material base for the traditional hierarchy of labour powers and so for the first time the possibility of the introduction of cheap unskilled labour on a large scale.

Along with the tool, the skill of the workman in handling it passes over to the machine. The capabilities of the tool are emancipated from the restraints that are inseparable from human labour-power. Thereby the technical foundation on which is based the division of labour in Manufacture, is swept away. Hence, in the place of the hierarchy of specialised workmen that characterises manufacture, there steps, in the automatic factory, a tendency to equalise and reduce to one and the same level every kind of work that has to be done by the minders of the machines; in the place of the artificially produced differentia-

28

tions of the detail workmen, step the natural differences of age and sex.[36]

In this sense, modern industry was a direct challenge to the traditional sexual division of labour in social production. In the Lancashire textile industry, for instance, women and children were the earliest recruits into the factories. But in London the ways in which the labour power of women was utilized in the transition from manufacture to modern industry was more complicated, because that transition itself, when it was made at all, was made differently in each trade.

Some traditional areas of the London economy, the small, specialized and luxury trades for instance, which depended on proximity to their markets and skilled handicraftsmen, were not at all affected by modern industry. Indeed in a few cases, they had been only minimally affected by the transition from handicrafts to manufacture. There were still handfuls of women working in these skilled crafts – engraving, precious metals, instrument makers, watchmakers, etc. – who served as a reminder of the position that women had once occupied in production during the handicraft era. Yet even in the trades most directly affected by the industrial revolution there was no single process of adaption. Of those which had transferred to the factory, there were one or two in which the introduction of machinery at certain stages in the labour process was forcing a realignment in the sexual division of labour. In the Spitalfields silk industry, for example, William Wallis, a weaver, states that 'the winding is almost wholly done by machinery now consequently it is performed by girls only', and that '. . . winding under these circumstances obtains the best wage of any other branch of trade in Spitalfields'.[37] Further examples in book-binding, hatting and rope and sailcloth making are discussed in the following section. But, on the whole, those trades with a potential or actual mass market found the high costs of rent and fuel and its transportation in central London, made the introduction of machinery and factories quite impracticable. Other techniques with which to counter provincial factory and foreign competition were found. The large supply of cheap labour favoured the development of

29

sweated outwork and other slop-work, not modern industry proper.

Industrial Change in London 1830–50: Slop-work

The slop trades produced cheap ready-made goods for retail or wholesale shops, showrooms and warehouses, in the East and West Ends of London, and the City. They were based upon the same principle as that which permitted the introduction of machinery in cotton textiles, the breakdown of the skilled labour process into its semi- or un-skilled component parts. They depended upon the unlimited exploitation of an inexhaustible supply of cheap unskilled labour. Women and children formed the local basis of this labour force, as well as the pool of casual labour that had always belonged in London. But from the end of the Napoleonic Wars, this labour pool was swelled by growing numbers of immigrants from Ireland and the agricultural districts.[38] As the men sought work in the docks and the building industries, their wives and children flooded into the slop trades. Long hours, irregular employment and wages often below subsistence were the marks of these industries, as the wholesalers or 'warehousemen' adjusted the labour supply to fit the demands of the market.[39] A host of new techniques – scamping methods – were introduced which shortened the length of time it took to produce an article. The division of labour, and lowering standards of workmanship enabled the influx of unskilled labour. A shoemaker in Bethnal Green in the 1840s describes some of the effects of slop-work in his trade:

It is probable, that independent of apprentices, 200 additional hands are added to our already over-burdened trade yearly. Sewing boys soon learn the use of the knife. Plenty of poor men will offer to finish them for a pound and a month's work; and men, for a few shillings and a few weeks' work will teach other boys to sew. There are many of the wives of chamber-masters teach girls entirely to make children's work for a pound and a few months' work, and there are many in Bethnal Green who have learnt the business in this way. These teach some other members of their families, and then actually set up in business in opposition to those who taught them, and in cutting, offer

30

their work for sale at a much lower rate of profit; and shopkeepers in town and country, having circulars sent to solicit custom will have their goods from a warehouse that will serve them cheapest; then the warehouseman will have them cheap from the manufacturer; and he in his turn cuts down the wages of the work people, who fear to refuse offers at the warehouse price, knowing the low rate at which chamber-masters will serve the warehouse.[40]

In every slop trade, there were various middlemen between the warehouse or showroom, and the producer. The work was sub-contracted out to the lowest bidder, who was usually a small master or mistress; the sweater in tailoring and the other clothing trades, the chamber-master in men's, women's and children's shoemaking, the garret-master in dressing-case, work-box, writing-desk making and other branches of the fancy cabinet trade (which Mayhew described as among the worst trades even in Spitalfields and Bethnal Green). Outwork was an effective counter to factory competition because it saved on overheads, required small capital and isolated workers, thus preventing their effective organization. Small masters employed their wives and children, and apprentices or other workers more destitute than themselves, to assist them. By constant undercutting and all the methods of slop-work, wages sank beneath subsistence and the small master undermined his own livelihood.

This sort of 'domestic industry' had always existed beyond the skilled 'honourable' sectors of the London trades, but in the un-stable economy of the thirties and forties, even workers in the 'honourable' sectors felt threatened by the expansion of slop-work, and especially by its erosion of customary skill differen-tials. A journeyman tailor, for instance, describes the blurring of distinction between men's and women's work:

When I first began working at this branch there were but very few females employed in it; a few white waistcoats were given out to them, under the idea that women could make them cleaner than men – and so indeed they can. But since the last five years the sweaters have em-ployed females upon cloth, silk and satin waistcoats as well, and before that time the idea of a woman making a cloth waistcoat would have been scouted. But since the increase of the puffing and the sweating system, masters and sweaters have sought everywhere for such hands as would do the work below the regular ones. Hence the wife has been made to compete with the husband, and the daughter with the wife; they all learn the waistcoat business and must all get a living. If the man will not reduce the price of his labour to that of the female, why he must remain unemployed; and if the full-grown woman will not take the work at the same price as the young girl, why she must remain without any. The female hands I can confidently state, have been sought out and introduced to the business by the sweaters from a desire on their part continually to ferret out hands who will do the work cheaper than others.[41]

It is easy to see why the journeyman tailor, the shoemakers and indeed most of the workmen who spoke to Mayhew at the end of the 1840s, could attribute their lowered standard of life over the previous fifteen years to the influx of cheap labour. Many trades had bitterly fought (tailors' and woodworkers' strikes in 1834 for instance) and failed to resist the erosion of skills, work customs and wage rates in those years.[42] But their diagnosis was over-simple. The flow of unskilled labour into a trade was the *result* of the dissolution of a skill. This, and the opening up of mass markets was made possible by the strengthening and concentration of capital within a trade, generally in London in the form of the wholesale or retail warehouseman. In this way the skilled workman lost his bargaining power against capital.

But the income differential between men's and women's work did not simply measure the distance between skilled and unskilled. The idea of the family wage had been transferred onto the labour market with the male worker. Although few men's wages actually did provide for all the family, one of the marks of a 'society' man was supposed to be his ability to take home a family wage, and the *assumption* that a man had to support a family, whereas a woman did not, was echoed throughout all but the most casual reaches of the labour market. That this assumption was unjustified, is testified by the Statistical Society's inquiry in east London in 1848. There were 229 'unprotected' women compared with only 125 'single' men.

A glance at the table which shows their scanty earnings, and the numerous families which are dependent upon two thirds of them, will convey a sufficient idea of the position of moral as well as pecuniary difficulty in which they are placed. Some of the women included in this class are, indeed, widowed only by the abandonment of the husbands. All, however are living unprotected with families dependent on them.[43]

Women's casual status as an industrial reserve army for most of London's manufacturing trades was buttressed by the ideology of the family. The implications of this were far-reaching. Whereas the unskilled countrymen who flooded the slop trades were eventually organized, women workers remained almost entirely outside the trade union movement throughout the nineteenth century, and into the twentieth. Their position as home workers, slop-workers, sweated workers and cheap labour both made them difficult to organize, and reinforced the ideology which prohibited their organization. By excluding women from trade societies, men preserved their patriarchal authority at the expense of their industrial strength.

The sub-contracting and undercutting of slop-work which reduced so many London workers to near destitution in the thirties and forties, were as much part of the 'industrial revolution' then as the machinery and factories of Lancashire. And the employment of women and children at less than subsistence wages in the slop trades was as symptomatic of the concentration of capital and the maximization of profit within an industry as the mill girls in cotton textiles.

Hierarchy of the London Labour Market: Women's Skilled Work

In such a state of flux within the labour market it would be difficult to construct any hierarchy of employment. But since most women's work was lumped together at the bottom of the social and economic scale, stratifying it is almost impossible. There are none of the familiar landmarks which help us to assess the relative status of a working man on the labour market. Few women's skills had any scarcity value or socially recognized status. Most of them – food and clothing, and the service trades, for instance – had only been transferred to the market in the previous 150–200 years. They had no experience of combination,

33

no sacrosanct customs, no tradition of formal apprenticeship – all of which established a skill.[44]

What skilled work there was for women, however, fell into three categories: the exclusively female trades; women's work in the 'honourable' sectors of men's trades, and factory work. These are the occupations which, as far as we know, required some formal training, where the wages were relatively high for women's work, and where there was the possibility of secure employment.

Dressmaking and millinery

Dressmaking and millinery, were trades traditionally in the hands of women and they remained so throughout the nineteenth century. Mayhew distinguishes between the two branches of the trade:

> The dressmaker's work is confined to the making of ladies' dresses, including every kind of outwardly-worn gown or robe. The milliner's work is confined to making caps, bonnets, scarfs, and all outward attire worn by ladies other than the gown; the bonnets, however, which tax the skill of the milliners, are what are best known as 'made bonnets' – such as are constructed of velvet, satin, silk, muslin, or any other textile fabric. Straw bonnet making is carried on by a distinct class, and in separate establishments. The milliner, however, often trims a straw bonnet, affixing the ribbons, flowers, or other adornments. When the business is sufficiently large, one or more millinery hands are commonly kept solely to bonnet-making, those best skilled in that art being of course selected; but every efficient milliner so employed is expected to be expert also at cap-making, and at all the other branches of the trade. The milliner is accounted a more skilled labourer than the dressmaker.[45]

Dressmaking and millinery offered girls both a skill and respectability – a quality indispensible to the Victorian lower middle class. But when looked at more closely, we discover that the opportunities they offered were limited, and these available only to a select stratum.

No working-class household could afford the £30–50 premium which was the price of a two- to five-year apprenticeship in a respectable house. Most girls served their apprenticeship in the country and came to London to be 'improved' – a process which took another nine months to two years, and cost a further £10 to £15 fee, in a fashionable West End house. There were at least 15,000 dressmakers' and milliners' assistants employed in about 1,500 establishments in London in 1841, aged between fourteen and twenty-five. Only a few of these were indoor apprentices and 'improvers' in the first-rate houses. Mrs Eliza Hakewell, who, with her sister, had kept such an establishment at Lower Brook Street, Grosvenor Square, for the previous twenty years, employed six or seven 'improvers' (but no apprentices). She told the House of Lords Committee in 1854, that they were 'very respectable young people (who) would not like to mix with common young people. They were the daughters of clergymen and half-pay officers and of first-rate professions.' Mrs Hakewell added, 'I have had many officers' daughters, many young people of limited incomes and many who come up to learn to make their own clothes.'[46]

These girls obviously fall outside the scope of our survey. So do the first hands, showroom girls and fitters, all the women Mrs Hakewell describes as 'the first-rate talent'. But most dressmakers and milliners came from less elevated social backgrounds; they were either 'out-door apprentices' – that is, they paid no premium and received no wages; or else they were day workers employed for the season (February to July; October to Christmas) and paid perhaps £12–20 for the year. These workers, according to Mrs Hakewell were 'quite common people: little tradesmen's daughters', or even the daughters of the poor. As a young day worker who supported herself and her mother on the 7s. she earned for seven or eight months of the year (and 1s. 6d. a week average for the remainder) told Mayhew: 'There are several respectable tradesmen who get day work for their daughters, and who like that way of employing them better than in situations as assistants because their girls then sleep at home and earn nice pocket money or dress money by day work.' 'That,' she added, 'is a disadvantage to a young person like me who depends on her needle for her living.'[47]

All dressmakers' and milliners' assistants were excessively overworked. Ill-health often forced retirement from the trade. During the season an eighteen-hour day was the norm, and it was 'the common practice', Commissioner Grainger reported, 'on particular occasions such as drawing-rooms, wedding or mourning orders for work to be continued all night'.[48] The result was that girls working at this pitch from the ages of fourteen to sixteen, suffered from 'indigestion in its most severe forms, disturbance of the uterine actions, palpitation of the heart, pulmonary affections threatening consumption and various affections of the eyes', together with fainting and distortion of the spine. Consequently, many young girls who had families to retreat to, did so. Those that survived the rigours of their teens and twenties in the fashionable West End houses (distinguished, according to Mayhew, by the fact that they 'put out the skirts and served the ladies of the nobility rather than the gentry') moved down the social scale to the third- and fourth-rate houses 'where the skirts are made at home (and they) seldom work for gentlefolk, but are supported by the wives of tradesmen and mechanics'.[49]

Long hours, ill-health, and early retirement were the rewards of many of the 6,000 young women employed in the 'better class' house. 6s. to 8s. a week for a day worker was a respectable wage for a young working girl, but the cost of lodgings were high (not all lived with their parents), and a further expense was the obligation 'to go genteel in their clothes'. In this respect, milliners and dressmakers were on a par with the upper servants, the drapers, or the haberdashers' assistants of whom it was also said that they were 'remarkable for the gentility of their appearance and manners'. Dickens humorously evoked the aspirations of some of these young women in his description of the West End cigar shop in which young men were

lounging about, on round tubs and pipe boxes, in all the dignity of whiskers and gilt watch-guards; whispering soft nothings to the young lady in amber, with the large ear-rings, who, as she sits behind the counter in a blaze of adoration and gas light, is the admiration of all the female servants in the neighbourhood, and the envy of every milliner's apprentice within two miles round.[50]

We know little about the organization or work process of women's trades other than dressmaking and millinery, in this period. Sectors of embroidery, tambouring, lacemaking and

TREMENDOUS SACRIFICE !

THE BONNET-MAKER'S DREAM

Bubbles of the Year – Cheap Clothing

straw-hat making were among women's skills which required a recognized training. Two other apprenticed trades were pearl-stringing and haberdashery. Some laundry work was also skilled and highly paid, and small businesses were probably run by women. But the numbers of women's trades had declined. Many had passed into the hands of men in the previous hundred years. (Hairdressing, for instance, which had given 'many women in London genteel bread' in the eighteenth century, was taken over by Frenchmen by 1800.) Fewer women were able to set up in independent business because of the separation of workplace and home, and the increase in the scale of starting capital. Some sewing trades remained almost the only manufacture both managed and worked by women on any large-scale basis in the nineteenth century.

Ivy Pinchbeck describes the scope of an embroideress's business, which, she says, hardly changed between 1750 and 1850:

... Women in business as embroiderers were in a very different position from the sweated journeywomen who worked at home on the materials and patterns supplied to them. Sadlers, tailors and milliners were their customers as well as the general public, and for advertisement the more enterprising of them occasionally held exhibitions of all kinds of needlework, including the then popular pictures in silk and materials, for which there was a good demand in a day when needlework was so universal an occupation.[51]

Women's dressmaking and needlework trades suffered from the competition from slop-work perhaps more drastically than any other manufacturing trades. The needle was the staple employment for women in London – apart from domestic service – and remained so throughout the nineteenth century. Distressed needlewomen were a notorious problem of London life. Economic instability in the 1830s and 1840s accentuated the inherent seasonality of the work making the skilled needle-woman's living precarious. As slop-work increased, so did the numbers of out or home workers, and the embroideresses, sempstresses, tambourers, artificial flower makers, makers of fine and expensive shirts etc. could no longer rely on regular employ-ment, not even in the first-rate (fashionable West End) sectors of the trade. A saw-seller's wife who spoke to Mayhew, for instance, told him that she 'could earn 11s. and 12s.' a week when she 'got work as an embroideress', but 'at present she was at work braiding dresses for a dressmaker at 2½d. each. By hard work, and if she had not her baby to attend to, she could earn no more than 7½d. a day. As it was she did not earn 6d.'[52]

The 'Honourable' Trades

The second opportunity for women's skilled work lay in the 'honourable' sectors of the male trades. These women were very much in the minority; they were confined to a few specific skills; they were seldom, if ever, included in the trade societies; their wages were very much lower than the men's in the same trade and any encroachment on the traditional sexual division of labour within that trade was zealously resisted by the men. Women worked in the 'strong' men's trade in shoemaking, for instance, where the 'closer's work' which was 'light compared to that of maker' was principally in the hands of females, many of them wives and daughters of the workmen. Mayhew stressed that he was speaking of the workmen who 'in that part of the trade which I now treat of (the West End union trade) work at their own abodes . . .' He added that 'the most "skilled" portion of the labour is, however, almost always done by the man'.[53] In desk making, a branch of the woodworking trades, again our information comes from Mayhew;

> The journeyman executes the ink range, or the portion devoted to holding ink bottles, pens, pencils, wafers, etc., and indeed every portion of the work in a desk, excepting the 'lining' or covering of the 'flaps', or sloping portion prepared for writing. This 'lining' is done by females, and their average payment is 15d. a dozen. Desks now are generally 'lap-dovetailed'; that is, the side edges of the wood are made to lap over the adjoining portion of the desk. [54]

Women in the numerous branches of tailoring were sometimes apprenticed. Women were also employed in some leather manufactories, sewing goat-skins into bags, or as sewers and folders in book-binding, and trimmers and liners in hatting. There might well have been 'honourable' sectors of other trades which employed women, but our knowledge of women's work is still incomplete.

Book-binding

Respectability and gentility were the qualities which set bookbinding above domestic service or plain needlework as an occupation for girls in the nineteenth century. Commissioner Grainger approved of women's work in book-binding provided the employers complied with the demands of propriety. He found Messrs Collier & Son of Hatton Gardens, for example, a 'respectably conducted establishment', Mrs Mary Ann Golding, the forewoman, assuring him that her employer only kept on those who had been apprentices or learners as journeywomen 'if they conduct themselves properly'. The premises of Mr Horatio Riley of St John's Street on the other hand, were 'rather confined'. Nevertheless, the sexes were kept apart. 'The females work in a separate apartment', and there were 'orders that the boys should not go into this room. There is a discreet person as forewoman in the shop.' Unfortunately, there was only one privy for the whole establishment, but Mr Riley was 'convinced of the importance of having separate privies and (he intended) to make an alteration to effect that object'.[55]

Messrs Westley and Clark, of Shoemakers' Row, also received special credit for the scrupulous care they exercised in 'reference to the character and conduct of the females in their extensive establishment'. 'A single act of levity, or even a look indicative of a light disposition', according to one authority,[56] was 'sure to be followed by the dismissal of the party.' Fortunately for the girls employed in other book-binding houses, this same scrupulous regard was apparently not to be met with everywhere.

Messrs Westley and Clark was the largest book-binding house in London, and was included in George Dodd's examination of London factory trades, *Days at the Factory*. It employed 200 women in folding and sewing whose weekly earnings ranged from 10s. to 18s. A small number of girls were taken on as learners each year, paid no premium the first year, and became journeywomen after two years, aged fourteen. Most houses were

41

much smaller, employing only six or so 'learners', and perhaps a few apprentices. The apprentices in the better houses were always boys, who were taught the entire trade for a premium (£25 at Messrs Collier) over a period of seven years. The 'learners' were girls who, according to Mr Collier himself, 'come for about nine months, paying a small premium of two guineas to remunerate the forewoman, who loses a good deal of time in instructing them'. In the lesser establishments it is difficult to distinguish between the apprentices and learners, both of whom served a nine-month or two-year term, and were often girls. Mr Collier went on to describe the lesser

parties in the trade who principally or entirely carry on their business by apprentices and learners; in some cases the former are boarded and lodged, and they receive very small wages during the apprenticeship, and in many cases are imperfectly taught the business; the learners, also, are only instructed in the more common part of the work. At the end of the term it often happens that the boys and young women are dismissed, because the master, doing the work at a low price, cannot afford to pay journeymen's wages . . . (He) has very frequently had occasion to dismiss women, who have been in such places of business, on account of incompetence. Has in some cases received a premium from parties who have been with small masters, and who have had again to work for some months without pay. Has had frequent complaints of the cruel way in which, in this respect, young women have been treated.[57]

Mr Collier was describing the 'dishonourable' section of the trade. One of the journeywomen at a second-rate house, Mr Cope's in St Martin's Lane, confirmed some of his claims.

Sarah Sweetman, eighteen years old.
Can read and write. Was formerly an apprentice for two years to learn the business; paid no premium; received 1s. 6d. a week; for the last three years has worked as a journeywoman. Mr Cope only executes a part of the business which belongs to the trade. There are some branches which he does not carry on. Apprentices here cannot learn all the branches; so that if they leave at the end of the term, they must go to some other house to learn the business thoroughly. In those houses where they teach all the business a premium is generally paid of 21 [£2] or 31.3s. [£3.3s.] and sometimes 51.5s. [£5.5s.] for six months; during which time they receive no wages.

42

Mr Cope's establishment was a second-rate house but not part of the slop trade, since he did not dismiss all his apprentices at the end of their term; most were employed afterwards as journeywomen and received 'wages according to their skill'. 'With regular work from 9 a.m. till 8 p.m. they can generally earn 12s. a week', Sarah Sweetman explained. But she had not been taught all the business, and would find it difficult to obtain another situation. She concluded that,

a girl who pays a premium for six months and has no wages, and who is thoroughly taught the business, is better off than one who is not taught the whole of the branches. Those who have been thoroughly instructed, can generally command profitable employment, which the latter cannot. If witness had known when she was bound that she should not have learned all the business, she would not have come here. A considerable part of Mr Cope's business, as far as the females are concerned, is carried on by apprentices; Several have left after they have been here a short time, some of the parents thinking the work too hard.

The average day in both large and small establishments was about eleven or twelve hours, allowing one or one and a half hours' break for lunch and tea, some returned home for meals. During the 'busy times' the work is carried on till

10 p.m., 12, 2, 3 and 4 in the morning. Has often worked all night; has done this twice in one week, but only on one occasion. The apprentices generally go home at 8 p.m., and sometimes they stay till 9, 10 and 11; on which occasions they receive extra pay.

Several other witnesses confirmed Sarah Sweetman's evidence, and the intervention of parents was often mentioned. Unlike the dressmakers and milliners whose family and friends either lived out of town, or else were too poor to influence the terms of their children's employment, the parents of book-binders' apprentices probably worked in the trade themselves and knew whether or not their children were receiving an adequate training.

Hatting

'It is a fortunate circumstance' wrote George Dodd halfway through his *Day at a Bookbinder's*, 'considering the very limited number of employments for females in this country, that there are several departments of book-binding within the scope of their ability.'[58] Hatting also offered 'reputable employment for females in the middle and humble ranks'. Dodd gave an account of Christy's, allegedly the largest hat factory in the world, which occupied 'two extensive ranges of buildings on opposite sides of Bermondsey Street, Southwark'. Just under two hundred 'females' were employed there in the early 1840s, and they earned between 10s. and 18s. a week, mostly in the manufacture of beaver hats which were fashionable at that time. Christy's was of particular interest since it offered 'some valuable hints' on 'how far female labour may be available in factories where the sub-division of employment is carried out on a complete scale'.

The degree of ingenuity required varies considerably, so as to give scope for different degrees of talent. Among the processes by which a beaver hat is produced, women and girls are employed in the following:— plucking the beaver skins; cropping off the fur; sorting various kinds of wool; plucking and cutting rabbit's wool; shearing the Nap of the blocked hat (in some cases); picking out defective fibres of fur; and trimming. Other departments of the factory, unconnected with the manufacture of beaver hats also give numerous employments to females.

Mr Dodd did not specify the ages, class background etc., of the women and girls, although he described the processes in which they were employed in some detail. He concluded that 'Where a uniform system of supervision and of kindness on the part of the proprietors is acted on, no unfavourable effects are to be feared from such an employment of females in a factory'. Indeed his descriptions of the 'trimmers' underlines this point for his readers –

We enter a large square room, full of litter and bustle, and find fifty or sixty young females employed in 'trimming' hats, that is, putting on the lining, the leather, the binding, etc. Some are sitting at long tables – some standing – others seated round a fire, with their work on their laps; but all plying the industrious needle, and earning an honourable subsistence.

Christy's, in the early 1840s, (like Westley & Clark in book-binding) was exceptional among hatteries. It coexisted alongside the workshops described by Mayhew in 1849 that were 'almost entirely confined to the Surrey side of the Thames, and until the last twenty years or thereabouts, was carried on chiefly in Bermondsey'. The 'tradesmen who supply the hatters with the materials of manufacture are still more thickly congregated in Bermondsey than elsewhere', and their numbers and variety imply that they were still in those years occupied in small separate workshop production, not combined under one roof as at Christy's. Women worked as hat binders, liners and trimmers; the subsidiary trades included hat lining makers, hat-trimming and buckle makers, as well as wool-staplers, hat-furriers, hat-curriers, hat block-makers, hat-druggists, hat-dyers, hat-bow-string makers, hat calico makers, hat box makers, hat-silk shag makers, and hat-brush makers. But Mayhew gives no account of women's work except in silk and velvet hats, which he claimed were 'now (1849) the great staple of the trade'.[59] No man was admitted to the 'fair' sector of hatting until he had served a seven-year apprenticeship, 'and no master, employing society men, can have whom he may choose "to put to the trade", and they must be regularly bound'. The number of apprentices was limited to two, whether the master had two or one hundred journeymen under his employ. Daughters of hatters were not formally 'bound' in this period; they probably received a similar form of training to the girls in book-binding. Hatters were generally married, Mayhew was told, and lived in the neighbourhood of the workshops. 'Some of the wives (of workmen in the "fair" sector) are employed as hat-binders and liners, but none,' Mayhew continues, 'work at slop work.'

Factory work

The division of labour between the sexes was successfully maintained when book-binding first entered the factory. But it was only much later in the century that the entire 'printing profession' was broken up into a score of different trades, and the subdivision of those trades into each of its detail processes, permitted the replacement of the skilled craftsman by the machine and/or 'cheap' labour. Then women and children moved into work which previously had been monopolized by men, but only into carefully demarcated work, modified by the male trade societies.[60]

Hatting has a similar history. Christy's hat factory, like Westley and Clark's book-bindery, combined under one roof many processes in the manufacture of an article.

It may excite surprise, [George Dodd warned his readers] to hear of saw-mills, and blacksmiths', turners', and carpenters' shops on the premises of a hat maker; but this is only one among many instances which might be adduced, in the economy of English manufactures, of centralisation, combined with division of labour, within the walls of one factory.[61]

But traditional skill differentials were maintained because the labour process itself had not yet been transformed by the introduction of machinery. Fur-pulling for example, remained women's work whether carried on at Christy's, or in the small workshops described by Mayhew.

Factories like Westley and Clark's or Christy's, for all the modernity which so impressed Dodd, were sophistications of the division of labour characteristic of manufacture rather than of modern industry. Every process in the manufacture of a hat was centralized under one roof. But the replacement of skilled workmen by machinery was rare.

One such change may be detected from Dodd's account of Christy's: women were in charge of the cutting and cropping machines. Mayhew did not mention women in this work in his account of small workshop production, so we may assume that the innovation was the result of a mechanization of the work process. Another isolated and striking example occurs in Dodd's description of a rope and sailcloth factory in Limehouse.

Dodd first of all describes 'all which precedes the actual weaving', which was 'effected in one large apartment; and a remarkable apartment this is, both in reference to its general appearance, and to the nature of the processes carried on therein'. Here, women were employed on the quilling machines, work in which they and children had always been employed even before it was mechanized.

The quill-machines, . . . each of which is attended by one woman have a considerable number of quills arranged in a row, and made to rotate rapidly. In the act of rotation the quills draw off yarn gradually from reels on which it had previously been wound; and the women renew the quills and the reels as fast as the one are filled and the other emptied . . . The little quills in the quill-machine, rapidly revolving and feeding themselves with yarn, require but little care from the attendant, who can manage a whole machine full of them at one time.

The much more complicated process of preparing the yarns for the 'warp' of the weaver elicited the utmost admiration from Mr Dodd, but he does not specify whether the work was performed by women or not. Most significant, however, was the employ-ment of women on the power-looms. Hand-loom weaving tradi-tionally was men's work, but in every branch of the textile in-dustry, women were replacing men, as machines were introduced and dispensed with the need for strength and skill. In Limehouse, for instance:

Forty of these, [power-looms] . . . are at work in the weaving room of the factory, and may from the noise they create, give a foretaste of the giant establishments at Manchester. The machine throws its own shuttle, moves its own assemblage of warp-threads, drives up the weft-threads as fast as they are thrown, and winds the woven canvas on a roller. One woman is able to manage two power-looms, to supply warp and weft, mend broken threads, and remove the finished material.

But even in sailcloth manufacture, industrialization was not complete. In this factory some men still operated hand-looms, and Dodd's account of that process contrasts strongly with the relative simplicity of the operation of the power-loom. Dodd marvelled at the

patience with which a man can sit for hours at a time throwing a shuttle alternately with his right hand and his left, moving a suspended bar alternately to and from him, and treading alternately on a lever with one or the other foot; and many have perhaps pondered how many movements of hand, arm, and foot must be made before a shilling can be earned.

Girls in the quilling factories in Spitalfields were among the highest-paid workers in the silk industry in the 1840s, where depression had reduced the hand-loom weaver's wage to 5s. 6d. in 1849. Their relative affluence was displayed in the 'bonnets with showy ribbons, the ear-drops, the red coral necklaces of four or five strings, the bracelets and other finery in which (they) appeared on Easter Monday at Greenwich Fair'.[62]

Lint scraping was also mechanized and operated by young girls who often came from the parish, and were paid 11s. to 14s. a week after apprenticeship for a twelve-hour day and one and a half hours for meals.

The attention of the Children's Commission was drawn to the trade by an 'opinion prevailing' that the children lost the use of their fingers and contracted consumption from the occupation. The witnesses were reluctant to offer such information, however.

An article in *Household Words* tells us that fifteen girls, fifty boys and eleven men were at work in the Lucifer manufactory in Finsbury in 1851. There is no account of the girls' work in the Finsbury factory, but at the lofty and spacious one in Bow, 'Swift-fingered maidens – aged from about twelve to twenty – can earn nine shillings a week, or even more; the slowest fingers earning about six', distributing the untipped tapers into frames.[63]

Topping and button-hole making in slop-work was generally done in the factory, but only because the employers feared their low wages would induce women to pawn the clothing if they were permitted to take them home. 'There is a large workshop called the factory, connected with each slop-shop emporium, and in some of them there are over two hundred hands at work' the author of 'Transfer Your Custom'[64] tells us.

Perhaps further examples of women's factory work tucked away in odd corners of the labour market would emerge in the course of research. But it is unlikely if the diligent Children's Commissioners didn't uncover them. The most important invention to affect women's work in London during the nineteenth century was the sewing machine. But it did not necessarily involve the transference of the clothing industries into factories, usually, on the contrary, it revolutionized the productivity of female waged work within the home. Indeed the effects of modern industry on the London trades in the nineteenth century were neither so uniform nor so *revolutionary* in terms of the sexual division of labour as many contemporaries, including Marx and Engels, had anticipated. Machinery and other changes in the production process were introduced piecemeal and distributed unevenly, and innovation was related as much to the supply flexibility and available skills of the labour market as to the technical requirements and possibilities within each trade.

Women's Unskilled and Casual Work

The problems of uncovering women's skilled work dwindle into insignificance once we move outside those carefully delineated domains into the vast uncharted world of unskilled and casual employment. Most women were casual workers in the sense that their employment was irregular, or seasonal, or both, and the boundaries between trades were indeterminate as women moved in and out of work according to their changing circumstances. Whether she lived alone, with a man, or with her family, whether she was widowed or abandoned, whether her husband drank, the number of children she bore, her age, all these things directly altered or interrupted a woman's working life to a much larger extent than they did a man's. This meant that there were few occupations a woman could enter and be sure of earning her living at it throughout her working life. It also meant that so much women's work tended to be the sort that was easy to pick up or put down – washing or mangling for instance, cleaning, folding, packing, stitching and sewing. It was for similar reasons that married women sought employment near their husband's work. The location of the man's trade determined the family home.[65]

A girl's working life might start very young – at five or six – helping her mother, minding a child, cleaning or sewing. An eight-year-old watercress seller had minded her aunt's baby when she was six. 'Before I had the baby,' she told Mayhew, 'I used to help mother, who was in the fur trade; and, if there was any slits in the fur, I'd sew them up. My mother learned me to needlework and knit when I was about five.'[66] Women continued working until illness or exhaustion prevented them.

Few London girls escaped a spell in domestic service. The

hierarchy of domestic servants from kitchen to ladies' maid in wealthy houses were often drawn from country estates, (like Rosa, Lady Dedlock's favourite in *Bleak House*). But servants of the tradesman and artisan classes came from among the London poor. Most working-class homes it seems, employed a young maid of all work, or a nursemaid, when both man and wife went *out* earning. The majority of children at Bethnal Green Market (held every Monday and Tuesday from 7 a.m. to 9 a.m.) were girls of seven and upwards who were hired by the week as nurses and servants mostly to weaver's families. Parish apprentices were similarly launched into 'industrial work'. Mr Fitch, vestry clerk in Southwark, informs us, for instance, that while the boys are apprenticed, 'principally to shoemakers and tailors, some to carvers and gilders, coachmakers, paper-makers, etc.' the girls 'go principally as servants, some as tambourers, straw-bonnet makers, etc; but in many of these cases they are principally occupied in household work'.[67] Other masters of workhouses or overseers gave similar accounts.

Going into service offered a girl food and shelter, as well as, if she was fortunate, the possibility of saving some money, which might later be used to set her sweetheart up in a trade. Loss of character, ill-health, inadequate clothing or marriage could all lose a girl her place. But washing, mangling, cleaning or scrubbing (floors, or pots and pans) was often taken up when necessary and available later on. The 1851 Census shows that the majority of general domestic servants were girls between fifteen and twenty-five, whereas the majority of charwomen, washerwomen, manglers and laundry keepers were middle aged and older. A woman who had worked as a mason in Ireland, for instance, 'cleaned and worked for a greengrocer, as they called him – he sold coals more than anything' when she came to England. But her daughter went into service till the fever forced her to pawn everything and left her too 'shabby' to find a place.[68]

The infinite gradations within domestic work were inform-ally measured by skill and respectability as well as income. A woman could earn 1/3d. to 2s. a day washing and charring. But as with most women's trades work was seldom regular, especi-ally in years of economic depression. A sixteen-year-old coster boy, brought up by his mother, told Mayhew that 'Mother used to be up and out very early washing in families – anything for a living. She was a good mother to us. We was left at home with the key of the room and some bread and butter for dinner,' but he went on – 'Afore she got into work – and it was a goodish long time – we was shocking hard up, and she pawned nigh everything.'[69] Washing and charring were both very hard physical work. Everything had to be done by hand and the working day was very long, from dawn till ten or eleven at night sometimes. The mother of an orphan street-seller 'took a cold at the washing and it went to her chest'; similarly, the widow of a sawyer told Mayhew that she took to washing and charring until 'My health broke six years ago, and I couldn't do hard work in washing, and I took to trotter-selling because one of my neighbours was that way, and told me how to go about it.' Laundresses and washerwomen were continually reprimanded, (as were shoe-makers), by conscientious city missionaries for Sabbath-breaking. But then a superintendent conceded that it was an occupation 'of so laborious a character, that the Sabbath is, in common with other days generally devoted to that kind of labour'.[70] Quite often a washerwoman's husband helped her with the mangling. The wife of a dock labourer, for instance, 'has a place she goes to work at. She has 3s. a week for washing, for charring, and for mangling: the party my wife works for has a mangle, and I go sometimes to help; for if she has got 6d. worth of washing to do at home then I go to turn the mangle for an hour instead of her – she's not strong enough.'[71] The income was much higher if the mangle belonged to the woman. An old watercress seller's wife earned 3s. a day taking 'in a little washing, and (keeping) a mangle. When I'm at home I turn the mangle for her', he told Mayhew.

A small laundry could be quite lucrative, and often employed several washing women. One street-seller was leaving the streets, she told Mayhew, because

I have an aunt, a laundress, because she was mother's sister, and I always helped her, and she taught me laundressing. I work for her three and sometimes four days a week now, because she's lost her daughter Ann, and I'm known as a good ironer. Another laundress will employ me next week, so I'm dropping the streets, as I can do far better.[72]

A 'respectable' laundress was paid 'about four shillings per dozen shirts, and one shilling per dozen small articles'. She pays her washing women 'from two shillings to two shillings and sixpence per day and her cronies from two shillings and sixpence to three shillings per day'.[73] Ironing, which was very skilled work, requiring careful handling of delicate materials and intricate fashions, was usually the highest paid in laundry work, receiving perhaps 15s. per week in these years.

The shopkeeping classes were as miscellaneous as those employed in domestic labour. Shopkeeping had always been women's work. The wives of small craftsmen or tradesmen traditionally handled the retail and financial side of the workshop. The Census lists women greengrocers, bakers, confectioners, dealers in vegetable foods, licensed victuallers, as well as a few grocers, tobacconists, drapers and stationers. There were also women dealers in timber, carriage building, etc., probably widows and relatively well off. A small general shop, like laundry work, was perfectly acceptable employment for the wife of a skilled workman. The most typical was the general, or chandler's store similar to the one patronized by a street sweeping gang in the Strand, which dealt in 'what we wants – tea and butter, or sugar, or broom – anythink we wants'.[74]

Street-selling was distinguished from shopkeeping by the fact that the goods were taken to the people, rather than the people seeking out the goods. It was an occupation that many women avoided unless they were born to it, because it was a hard life, and had the taint of poverty. Street-sellers eked out a precarious living, dependent on the spending power of the working classes. Work started with the early morning markets, and the street-seller sat at her pitch or walked the streets all day in all weathers.

Mayhew divides street-sellers into Irish women and English women. The latter he subdivided into four groups: firstly, the wives of street-sellers; secondly, mechanics' or labourers' wives who go out (while their husbands are at work) as a means of helping the family income; thirdly, widows of former street-sellers; and fourthly, single women. There was a sexual division of labour in street-selling too – women were principally engaged in selling fish (especially shrimps, sprats and oysters), fruit, vegetables (mainly sold by widows), and firescreens, ornaments, laces, millinery, artificial flowers, but-flowers, boots and stay-laces, or small wares: wash-leathers, towels, burnt linen, combs, bonnets, pin cushions, tea, coffee, rice-milk, curds and whey; also dolls, nuts, mats, twigs, anything cheap and small.[75] Stock was either bought from markets, swag-shops or other street-sellers, or the women made it at home. There were women street-sellers of crockery and glassware, too. They were called 'bart-erers' and usually worked in partnership with their husbands. The serviceableness of a woman helpmate in 'swopping', or bartering was great, according to one of the men of that trade.

The costermongers formed a distinct and irreligious commun-ity within London life, entertaining as they did 'the most im-perfect idea of the sanctity of marriage', and allowing their children to grow up with 'their only notions of wrong . . . formed by what the policeman will permit them to do'. Mayhew tells us that at about seven years of age the girls first go into the streets to sell.

A shallow basket is given to them, with about two shillings for stock money, and they hawk, according to the time of year, either oranges, apples, or violets; some begin their street education with the sale of water-cresses. The money earned by this means is strictly given to the parents . . .

Between four and five in the morning they have to leave home for the markets, and sell in the streets until about nine . . . they generally remain in the streets until about ten o'clock at night; many having done nothing during all that time but one meal of bread and butter and coffee, to enable them to support the fatigue of walking from street to street with the heavy basket on their heads. In the course of a day, some girls eat as much as a pound of bread, and very seldom get any meat, unless it be on a Sunday.

A coster-girl's courtship was usually short because 'the life is such a hard one', a girl explained to Mayhew, 'a girl is ready to get rid of a *little* of the labour at any price'.

They court for a time, going to raffles and 'gaffs' together, and then the affair is arranged. The girl tells her parents 'she's going to keep company with so-and-so', packs up what things she has, and goes at once without a word of remonstrance from either father or mother. A furnished room at about 4s. a week is taken, and the young couple begin life. The lad goes out as usual with his barrow, and the girl goes out with her basket often working harder for her lover than she had done for her parents.[76]

Costermongering proper was mainly a hereditary trade, but the wives of labourers went out selling, so did the children of the poor. The children sold oranges and water-cress – anything needing only a few pennies outlay. Old women resorted to street-selling to avoid the workhouse. Parishes often provided them with money or a small stock (for example bootlaces from the haberdashery swag-shops) to enable them to scrape a livelihood, relatives and friends donated the same. An old lady in the East End who had broken her hip when washing and walking in her pattens (clogs) had a basket of 'tapes, cottons, combs, braces, nutmeg-graters, and shaving glasses, with which she strove to keep her old dying husband from the workhouse'. Her husband was very sick now, but he 'used to go on errands' she told Mayhew, 'and buy my little things for me, on account of my being lame. We assisted one another you see'.[77]

Apart from domestic service, household work and the retail trades, women worked in manufacture. Mayhew's sensitive inquiries into 'poverty, low wages, and casual labour, its causes and consequences' in the 1840s uncovered the hitherto unrecognized extent of this work. He showed that the expansion of slopwork probably increased women's participation in the actual work-process of some trades – notably shoemaking, cabinetmaking and tailoring – especially with the increasing phenomenon of the small master.[78] The home of a woodworker, tailor, or shoemaker was transformed into a workshop and the entire family was employed in the production of the article. Woodworkers sold on spec to slaughter-houses, upholsterers, linendrapers, or warehouses; tailors, other clothing workers, and shoemakers worked on order from the shops and showrooms in the City and East End. Family work in these circumstances often became the last ditch stand of the worker pitched from the 'honourable' sector of his trade onto the casual labour market. The elderly Spitalfields garret master who made the tea caddies which he hawked to the slaughter-houses told Mayhew, 'My wife and family help me or I couldn't live. I have only one daughter now at home, and she and my wife line the work-boxes as you see.'[79] Tailors' wives fetched and carried the goods to and from the slop-seller; the wives of woodworkers went hawking. Sometimes the small master employed other workers besides his family:

In a small back room, about eight feet square, we found no fewer than seven workmen, with their coats and shoes off, seated cross-legged on the floor, busy stitching the different parts of different garments. The floor was strewn with sleeve-boards, irons, and snips of various coloured cloths. In one corner of the room was a turn-up bedstead, with the washed out chintz curtains drawn partly in front of it. Across a line which ran from one side of the apartment to the other were thrown coats, jackets, and cravats of the workmen. Inside the rusty grate was a hat, and on one of the hobs rested a pair of cloth boots; while leaning against the bars in front there stood a sack full of cuttings. Beside the workmen on the floor sat two good-looking girls – one cross-legged like the men – engaged in tailoring.[80]

The multiplication of small masters was a response to the opening up of cheap mass markets, and to economic hardship caused by the perilous fluctuations of the trade cycle. Both phenomena were integral to the Industrial Revolution. But family work, or small workshop production was not always the grinding struggle that it became in the worst years of economic recession. Piece-rates and work conditions varied to some extent with the skill and quality of the workmanship, and these were not entirely exclusive to the 'honourable' trades, in spite of the better bargaining position of workers in those sectors. Sometimes, the distinction between 'honourable' and 'dishonourable' simply described the division between the fashionable West End trade, and the city or East End warehouses. In toy-making for instance, the principal division was between those who made for the rich and those who made for the poor. And although the Spitalfields silk industry was suffering severely, as it always had done, from economic fluctuations in these years, pockets of family workers remained relatively securely employed.

When we speak of families [William Bresson told Commissioner Hickson in 1840], we must remember that in a family, when the trade is in a good state, there is invariably more than one loom employed. One man at a loom earns, perhaps, but 10s. in a week, but when able to employ the labour of his wife, children, or apprentices, perhaps three looms, and often four, are kept going, so that I cannot say. I know many families who, when in full work, earn, or might earn, 20s. per week. My son-in-law, for instance, lives with me in the house, and earns about 18s. This would be a poor sum for his family to live upon; but then his wife, my daughter, is very quick at the loom, and earns as much, or rather more, than he does himself.[81]

In spite of its decline in this period there were few trades, as William Bresson explained, 'in which a woman is able to earn as much as my daughter gets by working at the loom; although I must say', he added, 'it is a sort of slavery for a woman'.

The clothing trades offered most employment to women. Women worked in every branch of tailoring (outside the honourable sector) – on their own account as home-workers, or female sweaters, or with their husbands. Coats, waistcoats, vests, trousers and juvenile suits were in turn divided into different branches according to the section of the garment as well as to material, style, fit and quality, and payment was by the piece. The poorest slop-worker always had to find her own trimmings, thread, candles and coal. An old lady when employed 'at all kinds of work excepting the shirts' told Mayhew

I cannot earn more than 4s. 6d. to 5s. per week – let me sit from eight in the morning till ten every night; and out of that I shall have to pay 1s. 6d. for trimmings, and 6d. candles every week; so that altogether I earn about 3s. in the six days. But I don't earn that for there's the firing that you must have to press the work, and that will be 9d. a week, for you'll have to use half a hundred weight of coals. So that my clear earnings are a little bit more than 2s., say 2s. 3d. to 2s. 6d. every week.[82]

Trousers were her best paid work, they brought in 4s. 5d. a week clear, and shirt making was the worst, leaving only 2s. 3d. a week clear.

1849
NEEDLE MONEY

George Cruikshank

There were a multitude of skills concealed in the bald categories – needlewomen, seamstresses, or dressmaker. A pamphleteer wrote in the 1850s 'There is no style of cutting and fitting with which the intelligent seamstress is not perfectly well acquainted and must use her scissors in trimming and fitting.'[83] The Census (1851) lists over 43,000 dressmakers and milliners of whom the majority were outworkers. Those who received their work direct from the West End fashionable houses ('defined as those that put out the skirts') were mostly between twenty and thirty and lived in St Martins in the Fields, the Strand or St Giles, near by the houses. 'I know of no old woman who is a day worker in the superior trade.' A young day worker told Mayhew, 'You must be quick and have good sight.'[84] Others, working for the less exalted dressmaking establishments, or for the slop-trade, lived all over London (especially in the East End); they were all ages but were not necessarily paid lower wages.

All women's needle-work was very low paid. The West End out-worker was as exploited by the fashionable houses, as the East End labourer's wife was, by the showroom or warehouse – sometimes more so. Shirtmaking for the wholesale warehouses of the Minories was perhaps the least remunerative of the sewing trades, partly because the prices were undercut by the prisons, workhouses, and schools which produced shirts at starvation prices.[85] But government contract workers, who made the clothes for the army, navy, police, railway, customs and post office servants were even worse off. We learn from a maker of soldiers' trousers ('the Foot Guards principally'), that

The general class of people who work at it are old persons who have seen better days, and have nothing left but their needle to keep them and who *won't* apply for relief – their pride won't let them – their feelings object to it – they have a dread of becoming troublesome. The other parties are wives of labourers and those who leave off shirtmaking to come to this. There are many widows with young children, and they give them the seams to do, and so manage to prolong life, because they're afeared to die, and too honest to steal. The pressing part, which is half the work, is not fit for any female to do. I don't know but very few young girls – they're most of them women with families as I've seen – poor, struggling widows a many of 'em.[86]

More research might lift the clouds of almost unmitigated destitution which appears to have been the fate of practically all needlewomen in the 1830s and 1840s, indeed throughout the nineteenth century. Is it over-optimistic to imagine that some sewing performed at home, or in the small workshops scattered throughout the East and West Ends of London (as well as most of the suburbs), was less exhausting and demoralizing than the general image that the 'distressed needlewomen' evokes? Mrs Rowlandson's evidence for instance, to the Children's Employment Commission in 1841, while it exposes child labour, low pay, and long hours, reveals the different strata within the shirtmaking industry, and presents a slightly more dignified if severe aspect to some of the work.

No. 758. 19 July, 1841. Mrs Rowlandson
Executes orders for Messrs Silver and Co. Employs 50 women who make shirts, blouses, caps, collars, etc. These women work at their own houses, and many of them employ 2 or 3 hands each, some of whom are children. All the plain parts can be done by girls of 8 or 9, this is the usual age at which they begin. The regular hours are considered to be from 8 to 8; one hour and a half being allowed for dinner and tea. If an order requires it they work longer, but the children are never kept more than an hour, which is paid as overtime. Girls begin with 1s., in a week or so they have 1s. 6d., and increase to 2s. or 2s. 6d. as they improve. A good adult hand, if she has good work, can earn from 10s. to 12s. Employs at this time three sisters, who can earn as much if they have regular work, which is not always the case. For making the best shirts she pays 1s. 8d. to 1s. 10d. each, having herself 2d. to 4d. for cutting out, taking in to the warehouse, etc. Some mistresses charge as much as 6d. and 8d. for giving out the work; some of the workwomen have complained of this; it has lowered the wages very much.[87]

But Messrs Silver was one of the oldest warehouses in the City, and was conducted along marginally more reputable lines than many of the flash showrooms.

The clothing trades were the most overcrowded, but many others employed women home-workers, making boxes, brushes, brooms, envelopes, matches, mats, paper bags, silk stockings, umbrellas and sacks, engaged in fur pulling or card folding. Wages were paid by the piece, and work was irregular so that even the quickest hands were often very poor if there was no adult male wage-earner in the family.

Women with a little capital set up as small mistresses in other than needlework trades, in book-folding and binding for instance, and matchbox making. A small capital was necessary either to offer as security to the warehouse which gave out the work, or to get started on one's own. The most notorious method of raising capital was by taking on parish apprentices who paid a £5 premium.

*

I have distinguished between two principal areas of women's unskilled work – in the retail/service, and the manufacturing sectors of the London economy. But these were not strictly demarcated. Women moved easily from one to the other when their circumstances changed. There was the mother of the coster girl whose father 'used to do odd jobs with the gas pipes in the streets', who . . . 'when father's work got slack, if she had no employment charring, she'd say, "Now I'll go and buy a bushel of apples," and then she'd turn out and get a penny that way'.[88] There were the street milliners who 'have been ladies' maids, working milliners, and dressmakers, the wives of mechanics who have been driven to the streets, and who add to the means of the family by conducting a street-trade themselves, with a sprinkling from other classes'.[89] There was the ex-servant girl, married to a smith, who had once owned a house in the Commercial Road where they had let out lodgings. Misfortune reduced her to making 'a few women's plain morning-caps for servants', which she sold to a shopkeeper until that outlet dried up and she sold them herself at the New Cut.[90] There were the women who turned child minding for neighbours into a small Dame School. These received short shrift from the tidy minds of Benthamite educators. Fourteen in Bethnal Green were insultingly described by a British Schools Inspector thus:

> They are in general good for nothing. A broken down mechanic's wife, fit for nothing but the wash-tub, or perhaps as a last resource to keep her from the Poor-house, sets up a dame school and gets a few children about her, who learn scarcely anything.[91]

The inherent seasonality of the London trades accentuated the casual nature of most women's employments. But irregularity was not always oppressive; many London women workers took off in the summer months, for instance, to the market gardens and hop fields of Kent and Surrey. This unfettered anarchy of the female labour market gave women's work a sort of pre-industrial character strangely at odds in a self-consciously in-dustrial age. Even Mayhew seemed to chastize casual workers for simply being casual:

During the summer and the fine months of the spring and autumn, there are I am assured, one third of the London street sellers – male and female – 'tramping' the country ...

A large proportion go off to work in market-gardens, in the gathering of peas, beans, and the several fruits; in weeding, in hay-making, in the corn-harvest (when they will endeavour to obtain leave to glean if they are unemployed more profitably), and afterwards in the hopping. The women, however, thus seeking change of employment, are the ruder street-sellers, those who merely buy oranges at 4d. to sell at 6d., and who do not meddle with any calling mixed up with the necessity of skill in selection, or address in recommending. Of this half-vagrant class, many are not street-sellers usually, but are half prostitutes and half thieves, not unfrequently drinking all their earnings, while of the habitual female street-sellers, I do not think that drunkeness is now a very prevalent vice.[92]

Many women's employments merged almost imperceptibly into the many partial and residual forms of work which were the mark of poverty or even destitution. The dividing line as far as it existed, was determined not so much by the demands of the economy as by sickness, accidents, old age or the death of a husband or lover. The most frequent visitors to the night refuge in Playhouse-yard, Cripplegate, for instance, were 'needlewomen, servants, charwomen, gardenwomen, sellers of laces in the street and occasionally a beggar woman'.[93] Into this amorphous residuum were tossed all those occupations which respectable Victorians identified with 'vagrancy' and 'vice' – slop-workers, hawkers, trampers, street-sweepers, mudlarks, the inmates of lodging houses, the pickpockets who slept in the baskets and offal around Covent Garden. 'We can take nearly a hundred of them', a Covent Garden policeman told a parliamentary committee in 1828, 'particularly at the time the oranges are about. They come there picking up the bits of oranges, both boys and girls, and there are prostitutes at eleven, twelve and thirteen years of age.'[94]

Prostitution or the workhouse were immanent and real threats to the unsupported woman without a trade in periods of economic distress, and prostitution was often the chosen, desperate alternative to the workhouse. There is no space here to sketch the multifarious wealth of ingenious and pathetic forms of clinging to a livelihood, nor to trace the twists of fortune that regularly deposited the women in these twilight regions of the labour market. Let one 'needlewoman' rescued for posterity by Henry Mayhew speak for all of them.

I am a tailoress, and I was brought to ruin by the foreman of the work, by whom I had a child. Whilst I could make an appearance I had to work, but as soon as I was unable to do so I lost it. I had an afflicted mother to support . . . I went on so for some months and we were half starved . . . I could only earn from 5s. to 6s. a week to support three of us, and out of that I had 1s. 6d. to pay for rent, and the trimmings to buy which cost me 1s. a week full. I went on till I could go on no longer, and we were turned out into the street because we could not pay the rent – me and my child; but a friend took my mother . . . . At last of all I met a young man, a tailor, and he offered to get me work for his own base purposes. I worked for him . . . till I was in the family way again. I worked till I was within two months of my confinement. I had 1s. a day and I took a wretched kitchen at 1s. a week, and 2s. I had to pay to have child minded when I went to work. My mother went into the house, but I took her out again, she was so wretched and she thought she could mind the child. In this condition we were all starving together . . . . (my mother) died through a horror of going into the workhouse. I was without a home. I worked till I was within two months of my confinement, and then I walked the streets for six weeks, with my child in my arms.

At last I went into Wapping Union . . . [where both children died in the workhouse].

I came out again and went into a situation. I remained in that situation fourteen months, when I was offered some work by a friend, and I have been at that work ever since. I have a hard living, and I earn from 4s. 6d. to 5s. a week. My children and mother are both dead.

The tailor never did anything for me. I worked for him and had 1s. a day . . . From seven in the morning till one or two o'clock I work at making waistcoats, and coats. I have 5d. a piece for double breasted waistcoats and coats, and 10d. and 11d. a piece for slop coats. I can assure you I can't get clothes or things to keep me in health. I never resorted to the streets since I had the second child.

Postscript

It seems premature to 'conclude' on the basis of research that remains preliminary. Nevertheless, this outline of women's work in London does highlight some neglected aspects of the 'industrial revolution' – in particular, the effect of that process on the sexual division of labour.

The industrial history of London in the nineteenth century demonstrates the strength of Marx's dictum that the capitalist mode of production revolutionizes the character of every manufacturing industry, whether or not modern industry is introduced. Machinery and the factory system were neither as universal nor as immediate in their application, as many had predicted in the 1830s and 1840s. Industrial transformation in London was characteristically expressed in the slop and sweated trades which resisted the factory throughout the nineteenth century, founded as they were on a minute division of labour and having at hand a plentiful supply of cheap manual labour. Women formed the basis of this labour supply. But women's position as wage workers extended beyond the manufacturing industries. Demand for female labour in the service and retail trades ebbed and flowed with the fluctuations of the trade cycle, and so – outside social production – did prostitutes, thieves and other 'fallen women'. Needlewomen and other home workers, small mistresses and their apprentices, charwomen and maids of all work, fit uneasily into the conventional image of 'the working class', but these were the expanding areas of the female labour market in nineteenth-century London; and in none of these trades and occupations were women's wages ever high enough to secure for them and their children economic independence from men.

Throughout the nineteenth and twentieth centuries, amid all the technical changes within trades as well as the industrial transformation of London as a whole, a survey of women's work reveals the tenacity of the sexual division of labour – a division sustained by ideology not biology, an ideology whose material manifestation is embodied and reproduced within the family and then transferred from the family into social production. As technical innovation toppled or abolished old skills, new ones replaced them, creating yet another male-dominated hierarchy of labour powers in trade after trade. It is the consistency of this articulation of the capitalist mode of production through a patriarchal family structure – even at the most volatile moments of industrial upheaval – which must form a central object of feminist historical research.

Notes

1. For a lucid statement of the purpose and need for a feminist history, see Anna Davin, 'Women and History', in Michelene Wandor (ed.), *The Body Politic*, Stage 1, 1971.

2. For accessible contemporary accounts of the breakdown of the family, see Leon Faucher, *Manchester in 1844*, Frank Cass, 1969, pp. 47–8; Frederick Engels, 'The Condition of the Working Class in England', *Marx and Engels on Britain*, Moscow, 1962, pp. 162–3, 174–82; for Marx's view of the material effects of modern industry on the family, see *Capital*, Dona Torr (ed.), vol. 1, Allen & Unwin, 1971, pp. 495–6.
3. Lord Shaftesbury was an Evangelical Tory and social reformer. His speech to the House of Commons, 7 June 1842, is cited in Ivy Pinchbeck, *Women Workers and the Industrial Revolution, 1750–1850*, Frank Cass, 1969, p. 267.
4. For contemporary views of the effects of density of population, see for example, John Simon, *Report on the Sanitary Condition of the City of London 1849–50*, p. 86.

> It is no uncommon thing, in a room of twelve foot square or less, to find three or four families *styed* together (perhaps with infectious diseases among them) filling the same space day and night – men, women and children, in the promiscuous intimacy of cattle. Of these inmates, it is mainly superfluous to observe, that in all offices of nature they are gregarious and public, that every instinct of personal or sexual decency is stifled, that every nakedness of life is uncovered.

5. Mrs Austin, *Two Lectures on Girls' Schools, and on the Training of Working Women*, 1857, p. 12. Hannah More (education), Elizabeth Fry (prisons), Mary Carpenter (Ragged Schools), Louisa Twining (workhouses), Octavia Hill (housing and charity reform) all advocated 'industrial training' in the form of housework and needlework for their 'fallen' sisters. These women opened up social work as an appropriate activity for middle-class women. Mrs Jameson's lecture, 'The Communion of Labour', 1855, was the most influential expression of the sentiments embodied in such activities. The links between evangelicalism, respectable philanthropy and early feminism have yet to be elucidated.
6. Charles Dickens, *Bleak House*, Household Ed. p. 56.
7. 1851 Census, vol. 3, Parliamentary Papers (PP), 1852–3, LXXXVIII, table 2, p. 8.
8. For seasonality and irregularity in the London trades in the nineteenth century, see Gareth Stedman Jones, *Outcast London*, Oxford University Press, 1971, chs. 1–5; H. Mayhew, *London Labour and the London Poor*, 4 volumes, vol. 2, 1861, pp. 297–323. On p. 322, Mayhew wrote, 'I am led to believe there is considerable truth in the statement lately put forward by the working

classes, that only one third of the operatives of this country are fully employed, while another third are partially employed, and the remaining third wholly unemployed'.

9. The preface to the 1841 Census stated that,

   the number of women about 20 years of age, without any occupation returned, consists generally of unmarried women living with their parents, and of the wives of professional men or shopkeepers, living upon the earnings, but not considered as carrying on the occupation of their husbands. (PP, 1844, XXVII, p. 9).

10. E. Thompson and E. Yeo, *The Unknown Mayhew*, The Merlin Press, 1971, p. 394. (Pelican, 1973). Henry Mayhew was a nineteenth-century journalist and friend of the poor. See footnote 78.

11. H. Mayhew, op. cit., vol. 3, p. 344.

12. E. Thompson and E. Yeo, op. cit., p. 407.

13. H. Mayhew, op. cit., vol. 3, p. 221: 'As a general rule I may remark that I find the society men of every trade comprise about one tenth of the whole .... if the non-society men are neither so skilful nor well-conducted as the others, at least they are quite as important a body from the fact that they constitute the main portion of the trade.' See E. Thompson and E. Yeo, op. cit., pp. 218–19, 409–10; Iorwerth Prothero, 'Chartism in London', *Past and Present*, no. 44, 1969; and E. Thompson, *The Making of the English Working Class*, Pelican 1968, p. 277.

14. H. Mayhew, op. cit., Vol. 2, p. 155. Mudlarks are

   compelled, in order to obtain the articles they seek, to wade sometimes up to their middle through the mud left on the shore by the retiring tide .... They may be seen of all ages from mere childhood to positive decrepitude, crawling among the barges at the various wharfs along the river .... mudlarks collect whatever they happen to find, such as coal, bits of old iron, rope, bones, and copper nails ... They sell to the poor.

15. Humphrey House, *The Dickens World*, Oxford University Press, 1961, p. 146.

16. Charles Dickens, *Our Mutual Friend*, Household Ed., p. 17.

17. Hector Gavin, *Sanitary Ramblings in Bethnal Green*, 1848, p. 11. See also Dr Mitchell's *Report on Handloom Weaving*, PP, 1840, XXIII, p. 239 for a description of housing in Bethnal Green.

18. Charles Dickens, *The Old Curiosity Shop*, Household Ed., p. 35.

19. Edwin Chadwick, *Report on the Sanitary Conditions of the Labouring Population of Great Britain*, 1842, p. 166.

20. *The Population Returns of 1831*, 1832, p. 14. These figures refer to the City within and without the walls.

21. Quoted in G. S. Jones, op. cit., p. 164 and see ch. 8. *passim.* See also K. Marx, op. cit., p. 674.

> Every unprejudiced observer sees that the greater the centralisation of the means of production, the greater is the corresponding heaping together of the labourers, within a given space; that therefore the swifter capitalistic accumulation, the more miserable are the dwellings of the working people. 'Improvements' of towns, accompanying the increase of wealth, by the demolition of badly built quarters, the erection of palaces for banks, warehouses &c, drive away the poor into even worse and more crowded hiding places.

22. 'Report of the Statistical Society on the Dwellings in Church Lane, St Giles's', *Journal of the Statistical Society of London*, vol. xi, 1848.
23. This estimate was constructed from R. Price-Williams, 'The Population of London 1801–1881', *Journal of the Royal Statistical Society of London*, 1885, no. 48, pp. 349–432.
24. J. Hollingshead, *Ragged London in 1861*, 1861, p. 143.
25. E. Thompson and E. Yeo, op. cit., p. 122.
26. Charles Dickens, *Old Curiosity Shop*, Household Ed., p. 57.
27. Derek Hudson (ed.), *Munby, Man of Two Worlds*, J. Murray, 1972, p. 99.
28. D. George, *London Life in the Eighteenth Century*, Kegan Paul, 1930, p. 170.
29. 'Report of an Investigation into the State of the Poorer Classes of St George's in the East', *Journal of the Statistical Society of London*, August 1848, p. 203. Of the women's occupations only one gunpolisher, one yeast maker, and one coal wharf keeper fall outside the conventional category of 'women's work'.
30. Handicraft guilds excluded division of labour within the workshop by their refusal to sell labour power as a commodity to the merchant capitalist. See K. Marx, op. cit., pp. 352–3.
31. ibid., p. 341. 'The collective labourer, formed by the combination of a number of detail labourers, is the machinery specially characteristic of the manufacturing period.'
32. ibid., pp. 342–3.
33. A. Clark, *Working Life of Women in the Seventeenth Century*, Frank Cass, 1968, especially pp. 154–61.
34. K. Marx, op. cit., p. 646.
35. See P. Laslett, *The World We Have Lost*, Methuen, 1971, ch. 1; A. Clark, op. cit., p. 156, for women and marriage. Spinning for example, women's most important industrial work in the manufacturing period was ideal 'employment for odd minutes and the mechanical character of its movements which made no great tax

on eye or brain, rendered it the most adaptable of all domestic arts to the necessities of the mother'. (ibid., p. 9.)

36. K. Marx, op. cit., p. 419.
37. Select Committee on Handloom Weavers, PP, 1834, X, q. 4359.
38. G. S. Jones, op. cit., ch. 4; Arthur Redford, *Labour Migration in England, 1800–50*, Manchester University Press, 1964, pp. 48–9, 137–9. In times of good trade, for instance in the Spitalfields silk industry, whole families were employed, and

> from the metropolis, the demand for labour goes into the country. All the old weavers are employed with their wives and families; agricultural labourers are engaged on every side, and everyone is urged to do all he can. Blemishes for which at other times a deduction from the wages would have been claimed, are now overlooked. Carts are sent round to the villages and hamlets, with the work, for the weavers, that time may not be lost in going to the warehouse to carry home or take out work. (PP, 1841, X, p. 18.)

39. Under- or un-employment was one of the features of the industrial reserve army of labour, since the demand for labour-power followed the fluctuations of the trade cycle. See Marx, op. cit., ch. 25, section 3. In those trades which had not been transformed by the factory system and machinery, lengthening of the working day and the reduction of wages below subsistence were the only means of increasing the productiveness of labour and hence surplus value. See ibid., pp. 302–3, 475, 484, 658–9.
40. H. Mayhew, op. cit., vol. 2, p. 312.
41. H. Mayhew, op. cit., vol. 2, p. 314.
42. An analysis of the role of women in these struggles is to be found in Barbara Taylor, *Women Workers and the Grand National Consolidated Trades' Union*, unpublished paper, 1974.
43. Statistical Society Journal, op. cit., p. 203.
44. K. Marx, op. cit., p. 179.

> The distinction between skilled and unskilled labour rests in part on pure illusion, or, to say the least, on distinctions which have long since ceased to be real, and that survive only by virtue of a traditional convention; in part on the helpless condition of some groups of the working class, a condition that prevents them from exacting equally with the rest the value of their labour power.

45. E. Thompson and E. Yeo, op. cit., p. 518–9.
46. House of Lords Sessional Papers, 1854–5, vol. 5, p. 27.
47. E. Thompson and E. Yeo, op. cit., p. 525.
48. Mins. of Evidence, Children's Employment Commissioner, PP, 1843, XIV, f. 29.

49. E. Thompson and E. Yeo, op. cit., p. 528.
50. C. Dickens, *Sketches by Boz*, ch. III, 'Shops and Their Tenants', p. 28.
51. I. Pinchbeck, op. cit., vol. 1, p. 290.
52. H. Mayhew, op. cit., vol. 1, p. 363.
53. E. Thompson and E. Yeo, op. cit., p. 363.
54. ibid., p. 452.
55. PP, 1843, XIV, op. cit., ff. 242-3.
56. J. Grant, *Lights and Shadows of London Life*, vol. 1, 1842, p. 196.
57. PP, 1843, XIV, ff. 241-2, and following quotes from same source.
58. G. Dodds *Days at the Factory*, 1843, pp. 370-71, and following quotes from same source.
59. E. Thompson and E. Yeo, op. cit., p. 534.
60. J. R. MacDonald, *Women in the Printing Trades*, 1904, chs. 1 and 11. Summarizing the reasons why women replaced men, MacDonald wrote: 'The advantages of the woman worker are:
   1. That she will accept low wages; she usually works for about half the men's wages.
   2. That she is not a member of a Union, and is, therefore, more amenable to the will of the employer as the absolute rule of the workshop.
   3. That she is a steady worker (much emphasis must not be placed upon this, as the contrary is also alleged), and nimble at mechanical processes, such as folding and collecting sheets.
   4. That she will do odd jobs which lead to nothing.
   Her disadvantages are:
   1. That she has less technical skill than a man, and is not so useful all round.
   2. That she has less strength at work and has more broken time owing to bad health and, especially should she be married, domestic duties, and that her output is not so great as that of a man.
   3. That she is more liable to leave work just when she is getting most useful; or, expressing this in a general way, that there are more changes in a crowd of women workers than in a crowd of men workers.
   4. That employers object to mixed departments.'
61. G. Dodd, op. cit., p. 139, and following quotes from same source.
62. Dr Mitchell, *Report of Hand-Loom Weaving*, PP, 1840, XXIII, p. 271.
63. *Household Words*, 1852, vol. V, pp. 152-5.
64. 'Transfer Your Custom', London, 1857, p. 16.
65. C. Booth, *Life and Labour of the People of London*, 17 vols., 1902,

1st series, vol. 4, p. 299. Clara Collett wrote of women workers, 'the position of the married woman is what her husband makes it, whereas her industrial condition may depend largely upon her position and occupation before marriage'. (ibid., p. 298), and see ibid. for married women's lack of freedom of movement.

66. H. Mayhew, op. cit., vol. 1, p. 151.
67. PP, 1843, XIV, op. cit., f. 298.
68. H. Mayhew, op. cit., vol. 1, p. 466.
69. H. Mayhew, op. cit., vol. 1, p. 39.
70. *The City Mission Magazine*, vol. 10, 1836, p. 127.
71. H. Mayhew, op. cit., vol. 3, p. 307.
72. H. Mayhew, vol. 1, pp. 463–4. Kensal Green was apparently 'the paradise of laundresses', Mary Bayley, *Mended Homes and What Repaired Them*, 1861.
73. 'Transfer Your Custom', op. cit., 1857, p. 22.
74. H. Mayhew, op. cit., vol. 2, p. 496.
75. I have filled out Mayhew's list. H. Mayhew, op. cit., p. 457.
76. ibid., pp. 43–4.
77. H. Mayhew, op. cit., vol. 1, pp. 385–6.
78. Mayhew's investigations are invaluable because he allowed working people to describe their own lives, but he did promote the notion that women and children should be the economic dependents of their menfolk, as a solution to the 'superfluity' of casual labour. England was producing sufficient wealth to support all her population, he argued, but not enough employment. Women should therefore return to the home. This underlying assumption lead him to concentrate on men's casual labour rather than women's. His methods of investigation were very thorough however; see E. Thompson and E. Yeo, op. cit., pp. 61–2 for the detailed questions he asked of trade organizations etc., and read their introductory essays for an assessment of his work.
79. E. Thompson and E. Yeo, op. cit., p. 463.
80. ibid., p. 139.
81. Appendix to *Report on Condition of Hand-Loom Weavers*, PP, 1840, XXIV, p. 77.
82. E. Thompson and E. Yeo, op. cit., pp. 142–3.
83. 'Transfer Your Custom', op. cit., p. 11.
84. E. Thompson and E. Yeo, op. cit., pp. 525–6.
85. According to the vestry-clerk of the Stepney Union; in a letter to the Poor Law Commissioners: 'The Commissioners are probably aware that the indoor female paupers within this and the neighbouring unions, for many years past, have been principally em-

ployed in needlework, such as shirtmaking or slopwork, which is almost the only kind of employment open generally to females out of doors within this district, in which there are no manufactories employing female labour. To this resource they are almost invariably driven whenever deprived of husbands or of parents. PP, 1843, XIV, op. cit., p. 124.

86. E. Thompson and E. Yeo, op. cit., p. 159.
87. PP, 1843, XIV, f. 270.
88. H. Mayhew, op. cit., vol. 1, p. 45.
89. ibid., p. 372.
90. ibid., pp. 464–5.
91. PP, 1840, XXIII, op. cit., p. 270. According to the 'Investigation into the Poorer Classes of St George's in the East', op. cit., p. 198, the children observed by the Society were 'apparently very healthy' and sent as early as possible to school, 'though sometimes into little, filthy, smokey, dame schools'; others were 'clean and fairly ventilated, and kept by persons with habits of order and propriety'.
92. H. Mayhew, op. cit., vol. 1, pp. 462–3.
93. ibid., vol. 3, p. 410.
94. Mins. of Evidence, Select Committee on Police of the Metropolis, PP, 1828, vol. 6, p. 31.

ц 3-15